Wrested Scriptures Made Plain

Or:

Help for Holiness Skeptics

by

W. E. Shepard, Evangelist

First Fruits Press
Wilmore, Kentucky
c2015

Wrested Scriptures Made Plain, or, Help for Holiness Skeptics, by W.E. Shepard.
First Fruits Press, ©2015
Previously published: Louisville, Ky. : Pentecostal Publishing Company, ©1900.

ISBN: 9781621712312 (print), 9781621712329 (digital), 9781621712336 (kindle)

Digital version at http://place.asburyseminary.edu/firstfruitsheritagematerial/103/

First Fruits Press is a digital imprint of the Asbury Theological Seminary, B.L. Fisher Library. Asbury Theological Seminary is the legal owner of the material previously published by the Pentecostal Publishing Co. and reserves the right to release new editions of this material as well as new material produced by Asbury Theological Seminary. Its publications are available for noncommercial and educational uses, such as research, teaching and private study. First Fruits Press has licensed the digital version of this work under the Creative Commons Attribution Noncommercial 3.0 United States License. To view a copy of this license, visit http://creativecommons.org/licenses/by-nc/3.0/us/.

For all other uses, contact:

First Fruits Press
B.L. Fisher Library
Asbury Theological Seminary
204 N. Lexington Ave.
Wilmore, KY 40390
http://place.asburyseminary.edu/firstfruits

Shepard, W. E. (William Edward), 1862-
    Wrested scriptures made plain, or, Help for holiness skeptics / by W.E. Shepard.
    174 pages ; 21 cm.
    Wilmore, Ky. : First Fruits Press, ©2015.
    Reprint. Previously published: Louisville, Ky. : Pentecostal Publishing Company, ©1900.
ISBN: 9781621712312 (pbk.)
    1. Holiness. 2. Sanctification. I. Title. II. Help for holiness skeptics.
BT767 .S33 2015   239

Cover design by John Ramsey

asburyseminary.edu
800.2ASBURY
204 North Lexington Avenue
Wilmore, Kentucky 40390

First Fruits Press
The Academic Open Press of Asbury Theological Seminary
204 N. Lexington Ave., Wilmore, KY 40390
859-858-2236
first.fruits@asburyseminary.edu
asbury.to/firstfruits

WRESTED SCRIPTURES MADE PLAIN,

OR,

HELP FOR HOLINESS SKEPTICS.

BY

W. E. SHEPARD, Evangelist.

Author of Holiness Typology.

"As also in all his [Paul's] epistles, speaking in them of these things; in which are some things hard to be understood, which they that are unlearned and unstable wrest, as they do also the other scriptures, unto their own destruction."—II Peter 3:16.

PENTECOSTAL PUBLISHING COMPANY,
Louisville, Ky.

Copyrighted, 1900

By

Pentecostal Pub. Co.

PREFACE.

The wise man said: "Of making many books there is no end." We wonder what he would say in these days if he were living. Still they multiply, and we have ventured to throw out another into the stream of time.

Where there is a great need it is right to look for a supply. While many authors are writing valuable books on this great and important question of holiness, we know of no work that takes up the subject of these wrested Scriptures used by many in opposing this second work of grace. We trust that this little work may fill a place in this great field of full salvation.

All over the land objections are being raised against the possibility of living a sanctified life, and the Word of God is being sadly perverted to substantiate these errors. In this work we hope to accomplish three things: 1, to help those who resort to these texts, wresting them to "their own destruction;" we hope to clear away the fog that seems to hang around them, and by so doing to lead them into the true light; 2, to enable those who are in the sanctified life to see the Word clearly on these texts, and thus be saved from an overthrow of their faith; 3, and also to enable the sanctified ones to be a blessing to those who are in error.

Trusting that the Holy Spirit may bless the work on its mission of light, we send it forth into the world, asking all who may read it to pass it along and pray God to bless the good and overrule all mistakes.

W. E. S.

CONTENTS

CHAPTER I
If We Say We Have No Sin.............. PAGE 7

CHAPTER II.
There is None Righteous................. 13

CHAPTER III.
For There is no Man That Sinneth Not..... 23

CHAPTER IV.
Paul Not Perfect........................ 31

CHAPTER V.
Job Disclaiming Perfection............... 37

CHAPTER VI.
Paul the Chief of Sinners................ 43

CHAPTER VII.
I am Pure from My Sin... 52

CHAPTER VIII.
The Seventh Chapter of Romans........... 59

CHAPTER IX.
Paul's Thorn in the Flesh................ 74

CHAPTER X.
The Statements of Job's Comforters.......... 84

CHAPTER XI.
There is None Good but One.............. 92

CHAPTER XII.
Our Vile Body...................... 98

CHAPTER XIII.
I Die Daily....................... 104

CHAPTER XIV.
Be Ye Angry and Sin Not............... 109

CHAPTER XV.
Forgive us Our Sins................... 113

CHAPTER XVI.
I Keep Under my Body................. 127

CHAPTER XVII.
Be not Righteous Over Much............. 138

CHAPTER XVIII.
A Just Man Falleth Seven Times.......... 146

CHAPTER XIX.
I Have Seen an End of all Perfection....... 152

CHAPTER XX
Summary........................ 155

CHAPTER XXI.
Conclusion 165

CHAPTER I.

IF WE SAY WE HAVE NO SIN.

"If we say that we have no sin, we deceive ourselves, and the truth is not in us."—1 John 1:8.

The quotation of this text is used probably more than that of any other in the Bible in the attempt to refute the doctrine of holiness. Perhaps it would be better to say the attempted quotation, for few ever get it right, and we never knew one to give chapter and verse. It is generally quoted thus: "He that saith he liveth and sinneth not is a liar and the truth is not in him;" and that said over so very rapidly that one can scarcely catch the words. Perhaps this rapidity is due to its frequent use. "Practice makes perfect," and practice in thus repeating such texts makes perfect adepts in denouncing Christian perfection.

We are reminded of a certain lady who quoted these words to a young preacher, a friend of the writer, and was told that such a text was not in the Bible. She replied that it was in *her* Bible. In about two weeks or so the preacher asked her if she had found that text yet. She said she had read through the Psalms, the four Gospels, and most of the Epistles, and had not found it, but still declared, "It is there." One good result was that she got to reading her Bible.

If we take this verse away from its context it would seem to teach that it is self-deception for one to lay claim to freedom from sin. But is it honest to snatch a text, or a portion of one, from the context either to prove or refute a doctrine, when the tenor of Scripture teaches otherwise?

For one to take this text for a weapon against the experience or profession of holiness, proves that he is either ignorant of the Word of God, or else he is a designing man. If he is ignorant, he should not attempt to teach; if he is a designer, then he should be shunned.

If one is justified in taking a verse, or a part of the same, out of its place, then anything can be proved from the Bible. In one place it says, "There is no God;" but taking in the context it says, "The fool hath said in his heart, There is no God." Again we read, "Let him that stole, steal;" but when we read the whole verse it says, "Let him that stole, steal *no more*." Three verses below the one in question, the apostle John could be made to say, "My little children, these things write I unto you that ye sin." But who would have the audacity to say that John taught the people to sin? When we add the next word and read, "that ye sin *not*," we get just the opposite thought.

So it is with I John 1:8 and many other wrested Scriptures. Instead of teaching what opposers of holiness claim they do, they convey quite a different thought, and sometimes the very opposite.

What, then, does our text teach? Read the verse above, which is I John 1:7: "But if we walk in the light, as He is in the light, we have fellowship one with another, and the blood of Jesus Christ His Son cleanseth us from all sin." Suppose a garment were spotted with ink, and it were put through a process which *cleanseth from all ink,* how much ink would remain? Now, if a statement were made to the effect that there was no ink left, would there be any self-deception in that? On the same principle, then, if "the blood of Jesus Christ cleanseth us from all sin," how much sin is left? Then, if all sin is cleansed, where is the self-deception if a testimony should be given to that effect? Of course, we would not advocate self-righteousness nor self-exaltation, but on the contrary always put Jesus first, and let everybody know that all we are is through Christ Jesus. Instead of saying, "I am saved" and "I am sanctified," putting "I" first, say, "Jesus saves" and "Jesus sanctifies." Let the people see Jesus and not ourselves. We should be hidden away, but at the same time magnify what the Lord has done for us. Give Him all the glory.

To get at the true meaning of the verse in question, let us suppose a conversation between a Christian depending, as all must, on the blood of Christ for salvation, and a self-righteous sinner, who thinks he is good enough and has no sin, consequently no need of the cleansing blood.

Christian: My friend, did you know that "if we walk in the light as He is in the light, we have fellowship one with another, and the blood of Jesus Christ His Son cleanseth us from all sin?" I have proved this to be true, and if you will come to Him as I did you may prove it for yourself, and be cleansed from all sin.

Self-Righteous: But I have no sin to be cleansed away; I have no need of the blood of Jesus.

Christian: What? You say you have no sin? "If we say that we have no sin, we deceive ourselves, and the truth is not in us." Surely you are wrong and self-deceived. You should repent, confess your sins, and be saved, for we read in I John 1:9, "If we confess our sins, He is faithful and just to forgive us our sins, and to cleanse us from all unrighteousness."

Self-Righteous: But I have never sinned, and do not feel that I have anything to confess or repent of. I pay my honest debts, and treat my neighbors well, and support my family, and I believe I am just as good as any one. I am not a sinner, and have never done anything wrong.

Christian: Surely, in saying that, you are making God a liar, for in I John 1:10 it says: "**If we say that we have not sinned, we make Him a liar, and His word is not in us.**"

If We Say We Have No Sin.   11

Thus we get at the meaning of the last four verses of I John 1. The text in question, then, does not have any reference whatever to one who has been cleansed from all sin, but to one who says he has no sin to be cleansed from, when he really has sin in his heart. It is also just as applicable to the unsanctified Christian who denies the further need of cleansing.

Why should we turn lawyer and plead for sin as if the atonement was a failure and sin a necessity? How some people fly to these wrested Scriptures and there pillow their heads, and slumber on in their carnal security, when God is thundering in tones of Sinai, "Sin no more!" He is swinging the awful danger signal down the ages, "Stand in awe, and sin not."

What sad disappointment it brings to some people when God's prohibitions diametrically cross their carnal desires! And so they seek for comfort and ease in those misconstrued passages which will allow them to sin "just a little."

A professing Christian lady, living in the 7th chapter of Romans, doing things that she ought not, and leaving undone the things she ought to do, because she was carnal, sold under sin, and it was no more she that did it, but sin that dwelt in her—pleading her cause one day in a conversation with a sanctified lady, asked her to read a verse in the 7th chapter of Romans, as she supposed, for her vindication. The sanctified lady, knowing that she had made a mistake in the chapter and verse, nevertheless read the one cited, when lo, it read: "What shall we say then? Shall we continue in sin, that grace may abound? God forbid. How shall we that are dead to sin live any longer therein?" Whereupon the pleader for sin exclaimed, "That is not the verse I meant." An unsaved person, overhearing the conversation, spoke out and said, "Hold on! That's Bible, just the same."

Surely we have need of consistency; it is a great jewel.

CHAPTER II.

THERE IS NONE RIGHTEOUS.

"There is none righteous, no, not one."—Rom. 3:10.

Here we again face the necessity of studying the context to enable us to understand properly the meaning of a verse. To take out this segment of the text and declare that there is none righteous, no, not one, will at once entangle a person in such a snarl of contradiction that he will be hopelessly unable to extricate himself.

The word of God properly understood does not contradict itself. When we find some statement which is an apparent discrepancy, which flies in the face of the general tenor of the Scriptures, we should neither expose our ignorance in the wrong use of it, nor practice wrong in "handling the word of God deceitfully."

If, believing that it really means that there is none righteous in the world, we would place this portion of the text, "There is none righteous, no, not one," alongside of the practical teaching of God's word, we would at once find ourselves in a dilemma, and the odds would be against us.

Let us place by the side of it a few verses like the following:

"Little children, let no man deceive you; he that doeth righteousness is righteous, even as He is righteous."—I John 3:7.

It would seem from this text that John was warning them against those who claimed there were none righteous, declaring that "he that doeth righteousness *is* righteous."

"If ye know that He is righteous, ye know that every one that doeth righteousness is born of Him."—I John 2:29.

"And they (Zacharias and Elizabeth) were both righteous, walking in all the commandments and ordinances of the Lord blameless."—Luke 1:6.

"The effectual, fervent prayer of a righteous man availeth much."—Jas. 5:6.

"For verily I say unto you, That many prophets and righteous men have desired to see those things which ye see, and have not seen them."—Matt. 13:17.

Thus, we find that instead of there being none righteous, no, not one, the Word shows the number to be "many."

The Scriptures abound both in precept and in examples of righteousness. If the atonement of Jesus cannot make men righteous, we ask, What can it do? Our own righteousness, we confess, is "filthy rags," and Jesus said, "Except your righteousness shall exceed the righteousness of the scribes and Pharisees, ye shall in no case enter into the kingdom of heaven."—Matt. 5:20.

There is None Righteous. 15

We must have the inwrought righteousness of Christ. Not a robe simply, that covers our unrighteousness, leaving us sinful and unholy, but His righteousness imparted to us.

"If we confess our sins, He is faithful and just to forgive us our sins, and to cleanse us from all unrighteousness."—I John 1:9. If all unrighteousness is cleansed away, then certainly there is righteousness in its place. If the atonement of Christ cannot get down as deep as sin has gone, it must be a failure. But who would say that Christ made a failure in His atonement?

There is so much ignorance abroad in the land. So many seem to think that it makes very little difference if they do "sin a little." They claim that one cannot help sinning some every day in word, thought and deed. They forget, or else are awfully ignorant, that the Word is extremely prohibitory on that line. Hear the Word of the Lord:

"Stand in awe and sin not."—Psalm 4:4.

"Awake to righteousness and sin not."—I Cor. 15:34.

"Go and sin no more."—John 8:11.

"How shall we, that are dead to sin, live any longer therein?"—Rom. 6:2.

"He that committeth sin is of the devil."—I John 3:8.

"Whosoever is born of God doth not commit sin."—I John 3:9.

"Whosoever abideth in Him sinneth not."—I. John 3:6.

"The soul that sinneth, it shall die."—Ez. 4:18.

We fail to see how anybody can read such commands, warnings and assertions, and then fly in the face of them all and think that sin is of little consequence. Beware! "Be sure your sin will find you out."—Num. 32:23. One would better trifle with chain lightning than with sin. In view of the coming judgment, when the hearts of men will be weighed in the balances of divine justice, when sin will be sized up in its awful blackness and heinousness, let us see to it that none of the accursed thing be found upon our souls.

Sin and salvation are incompatible. They will not mix any more than oil and water. Saints cannot be sinners at the same time. One cannot live in the kingdom of God and the kingdom of the world simultaneously. We have read of "natural law in the spiritual world." The property of impenetrability obtains in the spiritual realm. Two bodies cannot occupy the same space at the same time. Neither can one body be in two places at the same time. One cannot be dwelling in the light of God and also be in darkness. He cannot be in the service of Christ and simultaneously in the service of sin.

"Thou shalt call His name Jesus, for He shall save His people from their sins."—Matt. 1:21. Not saved *in* one's sins, but *from* them. What is

There is None Righteous. 17

a sinner? Let us see. A liar is one who lies; a deceiver is one who deceives; a murderer is one who murders; a sinner must be one who sins. What is a Christian? A Mohammedan is a follower of Mohammed; a Confucianist is a follower of Confucius; a Christian is a follower of Christ. How did Christ act? He "was holy, harmless, undefiled and separate from sinners."—Heb. 7:26. "As He is, so are we in this world."—I John 4:17. Are we Christians? Are we followers of the meek and lowly Jesus? Are we imitators of that heavenly example? To say that one is a Christian and yet a sinner is about as ridiculous as to say that one is a truthful liar, an honest thief, an intelligent idiot, a healthy invalid, a living corpse, or a holy devil.

We are persuaded, though, that many times, when there is dispute on these questions, there is a greater difference in terms than in actual belief.

In the Old Testament we find sins of ignorance mentioned together with the necessary offering for such. They were not classed with wilful transgressions, and were dealt with in another manner. In the same sense may we speak of the same now, though the expression, "sins of ignorance," is not mentioned in the New Testament. We will always be liable and subject to mistakes, blunders and infirmities. We will do things ignorantly, which we will see afterwards, and for which we will be sorry. Yet these mistakes and blunders are not classed in the catalogue of sins. If they are, then everybody is a sinner, no matter what state of grace he has reached. They are all dead, for "the soul that sinneth, it shall die." They are not abiding in Him, for "he that abideth in Him sinneth not." They should not profess to be born again, for "whosoever is born of God doth not commit sin." It would make the Word of God irreconciliably contradictory. If those who claim to be Christians, and yet sinners, mean by sin, those things done in ignorance, we can accept their experience, but they should define themselves better. On the other hand, if they mean known sin, voluntary, wilful transgression, then we must believe them to be misguided and deceived. A thousand mistakes, or, to use the Old Testament expression, sins of ignorance, are compatible with the Christian life, but not any known, voluntary sin. The former will not break the union with Christ, but the latter severs the connection. Perhaps some mean that they commit known sin daily, but not voluntary sin. They have a quick temper, or some other weakness, which gets the advantage of them so suddenly that they are overcome before they think. They know it is wrong, but it is not voluntary. It is not with their consent, for they much prefer not to be overcome. They go at once to the Lord and ask pardon, but are overcome again and again the same way. Thus, they say they are Christians, but sin every day. Suppose they failed, after one of those spells, to find pardon, would they not remain in the dark? Certainly this is an up-and-down experience. We could not say an up-and-down Christian life, but rather an up-Christian and down-sinner life. Thank God there is a better way of going than this. God is able and willing to take the "down" element out of us. He proposes so to purify the heart that there will be no uprisings of unholy tempers in it.

We will take up the context under consideration and see if it is a fair description of a real Christian experience. If the portion, "there is none righteous," applies to the Christian, then certainly the context applies to the Christian also. We will take them in their order.

"There is none that understandeth, there is none that seeketh after God." If, then, there is none righteous, then none of them understand or seek after God.

"They are all gone out of the way, they are together become unprofitable; there is none that doeth good, no, not one." We must abide by the context; so, all Christians are gone out of the way, are unprofitable, and none of them do good, no, not one.

"Their throat is an open sepulcher; with their tongues they have used deceit; the poison of asps is under their lips." What a description of a Christian! His mouth an open sepulcher, using deceit with his tongue, and having the poison of asps under his lips.

"Whose mouth is full of cursing and bitterness." And this a Christian!

"Their feet are swift to shed blood." A dangerous class of people, that. All this applies to the Christian, if the first part does.

"Destruction and misery are in all their ways." All the ways of a Christian are destruction, and their lives are filled with misery. This is certainly a very dark picture, and not much in it to lure one on to embrace it.

"And the way of peace have they not known." Take the medicine, brother, if you claim that there is none righteous. There is no peace then in the Christian's heart or life. He has never known such a thing.

"There is no fear of God before their eyes." With a reckless, fearless, don't-care manner, he proceeds on the evil tenor of his way. All this applying to the followers of the Lord Jesus Christ.

Who, that professes to be a Christian, is willing to lay claim to such a catalogue of sins as his experience? If the first statement, "there is none righteous," applies to him, then all the rest apply to him also, for the subject is not changed until we come to the close of the clause, "there is no fear of God before their eyes."

A little further on it says, "For there is no difference, for all have sinned and come short of

There is None Righteous. 21

the glory of God." So, we see that it is simply showing forth man's condition in his unregenerate or sinful state.

Coming back to the beginning of this description, we find these words, "As it is written," and then follows that very accommodative text, with which so many have allowed the devil to morphine them. "It is written." Where is it written? These statements are taken from the 14th and 53d Psalms, and the 59th chapter of Isaiah. In all of these places the context makes it plain that the reference is to the unregenerate people. Especially does Isaiah make this plain. He says, "But your iniquities have separated between you and your God, and your sins have hid His face from you, that He will not hear." Then follows the place where it is written, as we see in Romans, 3d chapter. But that this is not a necessary experience, incapable of being overcome, the verse just preceding the one quoted from Isaiah says, "Behold, the Lord's hand is not shortened, that it cannot save; neither His ear heavy, that He will not hear."

This cuts off all escape, and leaves one without any excuse for pleading for unrighteousness. This catalogue of sins is arrayed against them because they have allowed sin to come in between them and God. But He declares that His hand is not too short to save nor His ear too deaf to hear.

The very fact that David, Isaiah and Paul all use this language to illustrate the sinner's life, proves that his heart is just the same, no matter when and where you find it. All the way down the ages it is just the same. There never was and never will be any improvement till it is improved by the cleansing blood of Jesus. The world is not growing any better, only as hearts come in contact with Him that is "mighty to save."

Dear reader, do not hide behind some refuge that will not stand the test of the judgment day. Beware how you plead for sin, lest you may not be able to pass muster on that great day of days.

CHAPTER III.

FOR THERE IS NO MAN THAT SINNETH NOT.

"If they sin against thee (for there is no man that sinneth not)."—I Kings 8:46; II Chron. 6:36.

"For there is not a just man upon earth, that doeth good, and sinneth not."—Eccl. 7:20.

To these texts we find a well beaten trail, filled with many weary travelers, like pilgrims to Mecca, "seeking rest and finding none."

Why should one find comfort in any statement concerning the sinning of Old Testament saints? Suppose there were none in those days who did not occasionally "miss the mark;" does that prove that in this Holy Ghost dispensation of Gospel light and truth, with an open Bible, illuminated with the Holy Spirit, and a present Savior, who came to "save His people from their sins," we have to "commit sin every day in word, thought and deed"? We must remember that we are living in a better day than they lived in. There are many places in the Word which show us that we have better privileges and opportunities than Old Testament saints had. The measure of one's light is the measure of his responsibility. The more light and opportunity we have the more will God require of us. The more grace we have in our hearts the easier can we live above the world and sin. Surely the grace of to-day exceeds that of Solomon's time. It is no excuse for us if those of former years did not do as they should have done. We are in a day of better things. We will notice some of these better conditions.

1. *A better Testament and better promises.* "But now hath He obtained a more excellent ministry, by how much also He is the mediator of a *better covenant* (Testament) which was established upon *better promises.*"

"For if that first covenant had been faultless, then should no place have been sought for the second."—Heb. 8:6-7. The New Testament and its promises, according to this Scripture, are better than the Old Testament and its promises. Not that they of the Old are false, but the New has more light and power and glory and salvation. We should not throw away the Old. It is helpful to-day. It did the work God intended it to perform in its day. But a new order of things has come. A new dispensation has burst in upon the world. The power of the Holy Ghost has come and brings in more light and glory. Adam Clarke, in speaking of this text, says: "His office of priesthood is more excellent than the Levitical; because the covenant is better, and established upon better promises; the old covenant referred to *earthly* things; the new covenant to *heavenly.* The old covenant had promises of *secular* good; the new covenant of spiritual and eternal blessings. As far as Christianity is preferable to Judaism; as far as Christ is preferable to Moses; as far as spiritual blessings are preferable to earthly blessings; and as far as the enjoyment of God throughout eternity is preferable to the communication of earthly good during time, so far does the new covenant exceed the old."

2. *A better hope.* "For the law made nothing perfect, but the bringing in of a *better hope* did; by the which we draw nigh unto God."—Heb. 7:19.

Everything in the realm of grace that is connected with this dispensation is more calculated for our betterment and salvation than things of the former dispensation. That was the shadow; this is the substance.

Adam Clarke says: *"The better hope,* which referred not to earthly, but to spiritual good, not to temporal, but eternal felicity, founded on the priesthood and atonement of Christ, was afterward introduced for the purpose of doing what the law could not do, and giving privileges and advantages which the law would not afford."

3. *A better salvation.* "For the law, having a shadow of good things to come, and not the very image of the things, can never, with those sacrifices which they offered year by year continually, make the comers thereunto perfect."—Heb. 10:1.

Contrasting this with Heb. 10:14, "For by one

offering He hath perfected forever them that are sanctified," we see that the possibilities of the old dispensation of grace fell far short of the grace to-day. The shadow of good things, with those sacrifices offered then, could not make the people perfect, says the apostle. But, here and now, under the offering of Jesus Christ, there is opened up a way for Christian perfection. So, we have a better salvation now than in Solomon's day.

Under this head Adam Clarke says: "Such is the *Gospel,* when compared with the *law;* such is *Christ,* when compared with *Aaron;* such is His *sacrifice,* when compared with the *Levitical offerings;* such is the *Gospel remission of sins* and *purification,* when compared with those afforded by the law; such is the Holy Ghost, ministered by the Gospel, when compared with its types and shadows in the Levitical service; such the *heavenly rest,* when compared with the *earthly Canaan.* Well, therefore, might the apostle say, *the law was only the shadow of good things to come.*"

Summing up, therefore, the facts that we have to-day a better testament, better promises, a better hope, and a better salvation, we are persuaded that we must live a better life than was expected of those who lived when Solomon spoke the words under consideration. That we have better things, to place it beyond any question of doubt, we refer to Heb. 11:40: "God having provided some better things for us." Then, if we have these better things, we should not measure ourselves with those of the other dispensation, who had so much less opportunity. Instead of hunting up some Old Testament loop-hole to crawl through, as an excuse for sinning, we should be where Paul could say to us as he did to those in Heb. 6:9: "But, beloved, we are persuaded better things of you, and things that accompany salvation, though we thus speak." Of course, when God has provided so much better things than those of old, He certainly would require better things of us. So, we say, What if it does say at that time, "For there is no man that sinneth not," it is no excuse for us to sin to-day. But some one may say, "Even if the standard was not so high then as now, they did not live up to their own requirements, for it says, "There is no man that sinneth not." Certainly, if they did not live up to their light, they would be counted sinners as well as we. But to say that Solomon meant that there was no one on earth but sinners in the sense of wilful transgressors, committing known sin constantly, is to fly in the face of all reason, as well as of the Word of God itself. If it be true that all were sinners in this sense, then there was not a saved person on earth. But we know that God did have His children on earth at that time. We might mention some, but any Bible student will call them to mind. Solomon himself was in a good state of grace when he made use of that statement. To say that there was not a person on earth in his natural state that did not commit sin would be true of that day, and also of ours. Or, to say that there were none that did not commit sins of ignorance would be true. Then, what did Solomon mean? We do not believe that he meant any of these classes: that there were none who did not commit known sin, or none in their natural state, or none who did not commit sins of ignorance. If these texts were rightly understood we are sure they would appear far different from what they now appear to many.

We are fully persuaded that Rev. Daniel Steele has given the proper exegesis of the texts in his book, "Love Enthroned." The following is his exposition: "Did not Solomon in prayer at the dedication of the temple (II Chron. 6:36) tell Jehovah that 'there is no man which sinneth not,' and does he not repeat the declaration in Eccl. 7:20, 'for there is not a just man on earth that doeth good and sinneth not"? We answer that Solomon, when correctly interpreted, as he is in the Vulgate, the Septuagint, and most of the ancient versions, gives no countenance to sin. These all read, 'may not sin.' The Hebrew language, having no potential mood, uses the indicative future instead. The context must determine the real meaning. The context is nonsense in King James' version, using an *if* where there is no room for a condition. 'If any man sin, for every man sins.' Let me illustrate the absurdity of this translation: At the laying of a corner stone of a lunatic asylum, the Governor in his address is made by the reporter to say, 'If any person in the Commonwealth is insane, for every person is insane, let him come here and be cared for.' We should all correct the blundering reporter and say *may* become insane, instead of *is* insane, in order to make the Governor talk sense. Correct the reporter, or translator rather, of Solomon and let him talk sense also, and you will hear him say, 'If any man sin, for there is no man who is impeccable, who may not sin.' This criticism applies to the quotation from Ecclesiastes also."

A note from Clarke's Commentary on this text from I Kings will give additional weight to the argument. He says:

"This text has been a wonderful stronghold for all who believe that there is no redemption from sin in this life; that no man can live without committing sin, and that we cannot be entirely freed from it till we die.

"1. The text speaks no such doctrine; it only speaks of the *possibility* of every man sinning, and this must be true of a state of *probation*.

"2. There is not another text in the divine records that is more to the purpose than this.

"3. The doctrine is flatly in contradiction to the design of the Gospel; for Jesus came to save

His people from their sins, and to destroy the works of the devil.

"4. It is a dangerous and destructive doctrine, and should be blotted out of every Christian's creed. There are too many who are seeking to excuse their crimes by all means in their power; and we need not embody their excuses in a creed to complete their deception by stating that their sins are unavoidable."

Surely there is enough in the Word to encourage any one to seek a better experience than a sinning religion. To seek to justify sin by the Word of God shows a very low state of religion, to say the least. To measure one's self by others, especially those of less opportunity, shows great weakness of Christian character. Christ is our pattern; He will lead us aright. Besides Him there are enough saints in all dispensations to incite any one to holy ambitions and purity of life and heart.

CHAPTER IV.

PAUL NOT PERFECT.

"Not as though I had already attained, either were already perfect."—Phil. 3:12.

Here we find the plain statement from the apostle Paul declaring that he was not already perfect.

These words are a soothing balm to those who would not for anything lay claim to perfection, and rather pride themselves in their humility and absence of profession, feeling, of course, that they would not be justified in claiming more than the apostle Paul. They say, "If Paul did not claim perfection, surely we ought not. If he was not perfect, then we are not."

Here is another place where the context must determine the meaning of the text. Let us throw aside all prejudice and get at Paul's true thought. When we read about perfection in the Word, we should inquire what kind of perfection is meant. We find different kinds mentioned, such as absolute, referring to God only; angelic, pertaining to angels; edenic, that state of Adam and Eve in Eden before the fall; resurrection, relating to our glorified state after the resurrection; and Christian perfection, pertaining to perfect love. Now, the question is, which kind did Paul have reference to when he said he had not yet attained to it? Let the context explain. "If by any means I might attain unto the resurrection of the dead."— v. 11. Here we have it—resurrection perfection. "Not as though I had already attained, either were already perfect."

Of course, he had not arrived at that state of perfection, because he was not yet dead and resurrected. Perhaps the question arises, Why should he be anxious about the resurrection, when all will be resurrected? King James' translation does not give the apostle's full meaning. The Revised Version more clearly sets it forth: "If by any means I may attain unto the resurrection *from* the dead." The true thought is, he wanted to attain to the resurrection out from among the dead. The apostle John writes in Rev. 20:4-6: "And they lived and reigned with Christ a thousand years. But the rest of the dead lived not again until the thousand years were finished. This is the first resurrection. Blessed and holy is he that hath part in the first resurrection."

Those who are so fortunate as to be in the first resurrection will be *from,* or out from among the dead, as Paul meant in the verse in question.

It is the holy ones who thus will be resurrected, and those who are not will remain dead a thousand years more. Thus, Paul was very desirous of being among the first to be brought forth from the

Paul Not Perfect. 33

grave. This is a strong argument *for* holiness instead of against it.

Paul was so intent on finishing his life thus that he was forgetting other things behind, and reaching forth to things before; and, like the racer in the games, he was pressing toward the mark for the prize of the high calling of God in Christ Jesus. Oh, that all would be as anxious to live holy lives as Paul, and thus expect a place in the first resurrection!

A further proof that Paul means the resurrection is found in Luke 13:32, where Jesus says, "And the third day I shall be perfected," meaning doubtless His resurrection. The same word precisely that Paul uses.

Instead of Paul inferring or teaching against Christian perfection, he suddenly bursts out with the declaration in a verse or two following, that he was perfect, meaning, of course, Christian perfection. Hear him: "Let us therefore as many as be perfect, be thus minded."—Phil. 3:15. There can be no mistake that in this verse Paul believes we may be perfect in some sense, not in the absolute. Not that we can be infallible. He immediately guards this point by adding in the same verse, "And if in anything ye be otherwise minded, God shall reveal even this unto you." And we find this to be true. In our earlier experience of perfect love we made many blunders and mistakes, but the gentle Spirit kept revealing them to us and made the way more and more plain as we continued to walk with God. Thus, some things which we did then through ignorance without feeling any guilt, we could not do now without condemnation, because of additional light. And no doubt we do things to-day which later on God will reveal to us to cease or we shall be condemned.

Surely there is a sense in which we may be perfect, or such admoniton would not occur so many times in the Word. Notice the following texts:

"Finally, brethren, farewell. Be perfect."—II Cor. 13:11.

"And this also we wish even your perfection."—II Cor. 13:9.

"Howbeit we speak wisdom among them that are perfect."—I Cor. 2:6.

"That we may present every man perfect in Christ Jesus."—Col. 1:28.

"That ye may stand perfect and complete in all the will of God."—Col. 4:12.

"That we might see your face and might perfect that which is lacking in your faith."—I Thess. 3:10.

"That the man of God may be perfect, throughly furnished unto all good works."—II Tim. 3:17.

"Make you perfect in every good work to do His will."—Heb. 13:21.

"That ye may be perfect and entire, wanting nothing."—James 1:4.

"If any man offend not in word, the same is a perfect man."—James 3:2.

"Herein is our love made perfect, that we may have boldness in the day of judgment."—I John 4:17.

"Therefore leaving the principles of the doctrine of Christ, let us go on unto perfection."—Heb. 6:1.

"Be ye therefore perfect, even as your Father which is in heaven is perfect."—Matt. 5:48.

What does all this perfection mean? It means simply this: We are to be perfect in our spheres as Christians, as God is perfect in His sphere. We are to fill our niche down here as He directs us. And in filling it we must have, through the grace of God, perfect love, perfect submission, perfect loyalty, perfect peace, and a perfect heart cleansing. Thank God for the possibility of Christian perfection.

How astonishing it is that people want everything perfect that pertains to this world, but are so willing to take salvation at such discounts! A lady goes into a millinery store, calls for a hat, and at once rejects anything that has a blemish on it. We call for a pair of shoes, and if there is something lacking we call for another pair. A farmer goes into a nursery and proposes to buy some young apple trees. If he detects woolly aphis or any other insect about the roots he will not take them. And who blames him? **People** want things right. They are not satisfied with anything short of it. God proposes to give us a perfect heart. Shall we repudiate His gift? Shall we ask for it to be discounted? Is it possible to obtain such a blessing as a perfect heart? "For the eyes of the Lord run to and fro throughout the whole earth, to show Himself strong in the behalf of them whose heart is perfect toward Him."—II Chron. 16:9. Such a blessing is for us, and we are a disappointment to the Donor if we fail to accept it.

We speak of other things that are perfect, and there is no fuss made about it at all. We find household articles branded "Perfection," and we think it is all right. Even tobacco will carry that name stamped upon it. If perchance Christians use it to designate God's article of salvation, immediately there is a hue and cry made, and they seem to think it almost blasphemy.

We pluck that lovely rose and say, "That is a perfect rose." We see that noble steed passing swiftly by and exclaim, "That is the acme of perfection!" We think nothing of it. If God is able to make a perfect horse or flower, is He not also able and willing to make a perfect Christian? "O, consistency, thou art a jewel!"

CHAPTER V.

JOB DISCLAIMING PERFECTION.

"If I justify myself, mine own mouth shall condemn me; if I say, I am perfect, it shall also prove me perverse.

"Though I were perfect, yet would I not know my soul; I would despise my life."—Job 9:20-21.

Looking at this statement of Job without taking into account the narrative, one would naturally suppose that Job laid no claim to perfection.

There are some people who seem to be more anxious to find something in the Bible *against* perfection than in favor of it. As a rule, people generally find what they are looking for. If they are hunting for flaws in Christian character, contradictions to holiness in the Bible, or discrepancies of other kinds, they can succeed satisfactorily to themselves. We know of a certain kind of bird that succeeds in finding enough putridity in this world to encourage its continual seeking. Yes, we can find what we are bent on finding. If we are searching for pure Christians they are around. If we want to find the way of holiness made plain and possible in the Word, there is no trouble to do it. If we want to reconcile those apparent contradictions in the Bible, all of this can be done.

If any one wants to get at Job's thought in the text before us he can do so. Instead of looking for license to do wrong or to live imperfect lives, we should strive to find out how we can better fill the niche in which we live.

We would not say that Job made a specialty of professing perfection, but we do claim that he did not deny the experience, as some would try to prove.

To understand him properly, we must take into consideration the awful afflictions through which he was passing. The news had come that his oxen, asses, sheep, camels, servants, sons and daughters were either destroyed or taken away. Then Satan covered him with boils from head to foot. One boil is sufficient to make some men boil, but here is one that is literally covered with them. It seems that his only earthly comfort was to crawl out on the ash pile and scrape himself with a potsherd. Then, to cap the climax, his wife turned on him and told him to "curse God, and die." But this is not all. Three men, purporting to be his friends, came to comfort him; and instead of doing so, they fell to accusing him, and gave him to understand that all his suffering and afflictions had come upon him because of his lack of purity and uprightness. He is told in the chapter previous to the one in question, "Behold, God will not cast away a perfect man, neither will He help the evil doers."—Chapter 8:20. That is, they would

Job Disclaiming Perfection. 39

inform him, that there was *prima facie* evidence that he was not perfect, or he would not be in the condition he was. Now, suppose Job had taken Bildad at his word and begun to tell the Lord that he *was* perfect, therefore by virtue of his perfection he should not be so apparently cast away and afflicted; thus, pleading his perfection as a reason why he should not undergo such troubles. We can readily see how it would condemn him and prove him perverse. But he finds no fault with God, and lays no claim to any goodness as immunity from suffering. Hence, he very humbly asserts, "If I justify myself, mine own mouth shall condemn me; if I say I am perfect, it shall also prove me perverse."

Surely it is very unwise and wrong for any Christian, no matter in what state of grace he is living, to tell the Lord that he is holy or perfect, therefore, because of his perfection, he ought not to be suffering affliction. Affliction, like rain, comes upon the just as well as upon the unjust. "Many are the afflictions of the righteous; but the Lord delivereth him out of them all."—Ps. 34:19.

Holiness does not furnish immunity from suffering or sorrow, and to plead so only proves one perverse.

Even if Job had in his humility refrained from professing any perfection, or even had ignorantly declared that he was not perfect, there is One who understood him far better than he understood himself, and whose testimony I would rather take than Job's. The Lord had previously settled that question beyond any peradventure, in the first chapter of Job and the very first verse: "There was a man in the land of Uz, whose name was Job; and that man was *perfect* and *upright,* and one that feared God, and eschewed evil." To make the fact doubly strong, He repeats the statement twice to Satan.

Now, if Satan, and Mrs. Job, and his "miserable comforters," and even Job himself, should all decide that perfection was an unknown quantity in his experience, I prefer to take the testimony of Him who knew. God said that he was perfect, and He cannot lie. The trouble with critics is, they confound Christian perfection with absolute perfection. They forget that Christian perfection may admit of mistakes and blunders, and that the absolute pertains only to God Himself.

But even after Job had made his statement disclaiming any perfection as a reason why he should not be afflicted, it would seem that he held up for the experience, intimating also that he was enjoying the same, and then stated just what we have been saying, that God allows the holy ones to suffer affliction as well as the unrighteous. Hear his declaration: "This is one thing, therefore I said it, He destroyeth the perfect and the wicked."—Verse 22.

Job Disclaiming Perfection.

Does the Word of God teach the possibility of perfection and give any examples of the same in Old Testament times? Let us see:

"Noah was a just man and perfect in his generations."—Gen. 6:9.

"I am the Almighty God; walk before me, and be thou perfect."—Gen. 17:1.

"Thou shalt be perfect with the Lord thy God."—Deut. 18:13.

"Mark the perfect man, and behold the upright; for the end of that man is peace."—Psalm 37:37.

"I will behave myself wisely in a perfect way."—Psalm 101:2.

"He that walketh in a perfect way, he shall serve me."—Psalm 101:6.

"Blessed are the perfect (see margin) in the way."—Psalm 119:1.

"For the upright shall dwell in the land, and the perfect shall remain in it."—Prov. 2:21.

"I beseech Thee, O Lord, remember now how I have walked before Thee in truth and with a perfect heart, and have done that which is good in Thy sight."—II Kings 20:3.

"For the eyes of the Lord run to and fro throughout the whole earth, to show Himself strong in the behalf of them whose heart is perfect toward Him."—II Chron. 16:9.

When we read such statements as these, we must certainly admit that there was not only a possibility, but a real experience of some kind of perfection in the Old Testament days. It is true that the standard of perfection may not have been as high as it is now, but that only puts more responsibility upon us, because of the greater privileges we enjoy.

If one has obtained what salvation God intended him to receive, and is living in the sphere in which He desires him to live, and is filling the niche that He has marked out for him to fill, that person then is regarded as a perfect man. Even if that salvation, or sphere, or niche in those Old Testament times did not mean as much as now, yet if any one measured up to the standard then he was counted a perfect man.

Surely God could not require any less of a person and be consistent with His nature and government.

CHAPTER VI.

PAUL THE CHIEF OF SINNERS.

"This is a faithful saying, and worthy of all acceptation, that Christ Jesus came into the world to save sinners; of whom I am chief."—I Tim. 1:15.

This verse is quoted to prove that no matter how much grace one has received from the Lord, yet he can never get beyond the place where he is reckoned a sinner. "If Paul said he was the chief of sinners, then how dare we, with so much less grace and salvation, lay claim to anything higher?"

Let us examine Paul a little. If he meant here that he, at this time, was the chief of sinners, let us see how this statement harmonizes with the rest of his teaching.

1. Paul was an apostle. He wrote upon one occasion that he supposed he "was not a whit behind the very chiefest apostles."—II Cor. 11:5. It is true that in his humility he said he was "less than the least of all saints," when he considered what a sinner he had been, and how the Lord had saved him and exalted him to preach "the unsearchable riches of Christ;" but even in this humble statement he confesses that he is a saint,

which means a holy person, and, to say the least, it is above being the chief of sinners.

He said that he was "allowed of God to be put in trust with the Gospel." We cannot understand how God could choose a man to be an apostle and commit unto him the Gospel to preach, knowing that he was the chief of sinners.

2. He wrote on another occasion that the mystery was "revealed unto the holy apostles."—Eph. 3:5. This, of course, included himself, as he was an apostle. Here is a profession of holiness from Paul. It sounds somewhat different from being the chief of sinners.

3. Paul told the Thessalonian church, "Ye are witnesses, and God also, how holily and justly and unblameably we behaved ourselves among you that believe."—I Thess. 2:10. Suppose that he had added in the next verse, that he was the chief of sinners, how would they have reconciled the statements?

4. In another place Paul made a profession of Christian perfection: "Let *us* therefore, as many as be perfect, be thus minded."—Phil. 3:15. Paul thus classes himself with those who had obtained this perfection. The chief of sinners would hardly harmonize in this place.

5. He wrote to the Romans and said: "I am sure, that when I come unto you, I shall come in the fulness of the blessing of the Gospel of Christ."—Rom. 15:29. How can one be in the

Paul the Chief of Sinners. 45

fulness of the blessing of Christ, and at the same time be the chief of sinners?

6. In another place he writes that he is crucified with Christ, and that Christ is living in him. —Gal. 2:20. One of the strongest expressions of full salvation. Is the chief of sinners crucified with Christ, and possessed with the Christ life?

7. He won hundreds to Christ and led many into the baptism with the Holy Ghost. How could one continually succeed in raising men to a higher level than himself? How could one, the chief of sinners, succeed in getting other sinners to God, and then in getting them filled with the Holy Ghost?

8. God trusted Paul to write a portion of the inspired Word; committed unto him a "dispensation of the Gospel;" through him wrought miracles of different kinds. Can we imagine a Holy God committing such sacred works to the chief of sinners?

9. The very next year after Paul wrote this text about the chief of sinners, he wrote: "For I am now ready to be offered, and the time of my departure is at hand. I have fought a good fight, I have finished my course, I have kept the faith; henceforth there is laid up for me a crown of righteousness, which the Lord, the righteous judge, shall give me at that day; and not to me only, but unto them also that love His appearing."—II Tim. 4:6-8. How could the chief of sinners say, as he

was facing death, that he had fought a good fight, and kept the faith, and was expecting a crown of righteousness? Is a crown of righteousness laid up for sinners?

10. Paul wrote, "Awake to righteousness, and sin not."—I Cor. 15:34. And again he asks the question, "What shall we say then? Shall we continue in sin that grace may abound? God forbid. How shall we, that are dead to sin, live any longer therein?"—Rom. 6:1-2. Strange that Paul should exhort others to quit sinning and keep right on himself. Where would be the consistency?

11. We read in the Word that "Sin is the transgression of the law." Also, "Therefore to him that knoweth to do good, and doeth it not, to him it is sin." Now, if Paul was the chief of sinners, then he was a transgressor of the law. This would prove hypocrisy in him—teaching others what he himself did not live up to. If he knew to do good and did it not, which he did if he were the chief of sinners, then how could he be holy, and just, and unblameable, as he declared he was? This would certainly brand him as false, if he were then the chief of sinners.

12. Long years before Paul wrote the text in question he repented of his sins. Christ met him on the road to Damascus, struck him down under a mighty load of conviction, and shortly he was a gloriously saved man. Every sin he ever com-

mitted was blotted out, to be remembered against him no more forever. Now, the question arises, If he were the chief of sinners at the time he wrote this text, did God give him a license to go back into the heinous business again, or did he deliberately take things into his own hands and go to sinning? If he were the chief of sinners, then we demand a solution.

13. Notice carefully the apostle John on sin:
"Whosoever abideth in him sinneth not; whosoever sinneth hath not seen him, neither known him."—I John 3:6.

"He that committeth sin is of the devil; for the devil sinneth from the beginning. For this purpose the Son of God was manifested, that he might destroy the works of the devil."—I John 3:8.

"Whosoever is born of God doth not commit sin; for his seed remaineth in him; and he cannot sin, because he is born of God."—I John 3:9.

If the apostle Paul was, at the time of that writing, the chief of sinners, then, according to the apostle John, he was not abiding in Christ, had not seen Him, nor known Him. But Paul declares to the contrary in all three of these things. Hear him:

"I knew a man *in Christ* above fourteen years ago," etc.—II Cor. 12:2. This man that Paul refers to is himself. See the context.

"Have I not *seen Jesus Christ* our Lord?"—I Cor. 9:1.

"I *know whom* I have believed."—II Tim. 1:12.

Thus, we see that Paul was in Christ; he had seen Him, and also knew Him.

Again, if the aspostle John was correct, and Paul was the chief of sinners, then he was of the devil, and had not had the works of the devil destroyed out of him. But to say this of such a man would be hard indeed.

Again, in the next place, according to John, Paul could not have been born of God, for such, John informs us, are not the chief of sinners.

He that would make out Paul as saying that he was at this time the chief of sinners, flies in the face of reason, of the Word of God, of Paul's own testimony and experience. He would make him to be not only false and hypocritical, but a deceiver.

But we know that it means something, for it is there. "Christ Jesus came into the world to save sinners; of whom I am chief." That Christ came to save sinners there is no dispute in orthodoxy. That he saved Paul is not a mooted question. That he was at one time the chief of sinners, all are willing to admit that in his humility he felt. That he was at the time of that writing such a character, either in thought or reality, is the "bone of contention." One may say that it was simply an expression of humility on the part of Paul in using the phrase, but there is too much at stake for one to make use of such an expression, so far out of the bounds of all truth, for humility's sake. What, then, does he mean? He means just what he says. He is speaking of two things that came into his life—one was sin, and the other was salvation. He calls attention to the fact of his being the chief of sinners, and as the chief of sinners Christ saved him, thus giving hope for others. If Christ could save the chief of sinners, then might all have hope. The word chief is mentioned simply to show the power of Christ's salvation. Notice the verse below: "For this cause I (the chief of sinners) obtained mercy." This power was brought to bear upon one who was the chief of sinners. But that power acted long years in the past at his conversion. Then the word "chief of sinners" must apply to the time when the power of salvation was exerted. Hence, we see that it was not at the time of that writing, but at the time of his conversion—not the chief sinner now, but the chief sinner saved then. It makes a great deal of difference when we wake up to the fact that he is writing of the chief sinner *saved* instead of the chief sinner still in his sins. It would be a poor salvation that left him still the chief of sinners. Adding a word or two to the text by way of explanation may throw light upon it: "This is a faithful saying, and worthy of all acceptation, that Christ Jesus came into the world to save sinners; of whom I am chief" (or, the chief one saved). Not now a chief sinner, but a chief saved one who was a sinner.

So that Paul, instead of lowering the standard, and confessing himself to be the chief of sinners, is doing the very opposite; confessing his great salvation, and showing that he is the chief saved one, by formerly being such a sinner, and now by having such a wonderful salvation.

One of the great delusions of the day is, that one may be a Christian, and at the same time be a sinner. Never did the devil hatch up a greater soul-deceiving lie. Even the expression, "I am a sinner, saved by grace," is not only misleading, but unscriptural. As some one has said, "They will emphasize the word *sinner* and whisper *saved.*" If one is a sinner, he is not saved. Of course, the majority may understand what one means by it, but the fact is, salvation and sin do not mix. To say, that I *was* a sinner, but am now saved by grace, would be the truth. If we stick to the Word of God there is no possible way to harmonize the two states—sin and salvation. There is as much propriety in saying, I am a liar, though truthful by grace; or, I am a corpse, alive by the power of God; or, I am a drunkard, made temperate by the gold cure; as to say, I am a sinner, saved by grace. The fact is, the expression is put in the present tense, when it should be in the past, showing when the work was done. If a

Paul the Chief of Sinners. 51

man is a corpse, he is not alive; if one is a liar, he is not truthful; if he is a drunkard, he is not temperate.

The word of God does not mix things. It puts them where they belong. If one is a sinner, he is not saved; he is of the devil, out of Christ and not born again. All of this John makes plain.

Why people want to hide behind some wrested Scripture to their soul's destruction, when there is so much light shed on the pathway, is a mystery indeed. May the Lord save the people from being sinners.

CHAPTER VII.

I AM PURE FROM MY SIN.

"Who can say I have made my heart clean, I am pure from my sin?"—*Prov. 20:9.*

This text certainly does not insinuate that it is impossible to obtain a pure heart or to be made pure from sin. But it does teach what the whole tenor of Scripture makes plain, that no man can save himself or purify his own heart. While each one can comply with the conditions of salvation and be saved, yet no one has the power to do the work himself. This great fact is made plain by that wonderful text of Jer. 13:23: "Can the Ethiopian change his skin, or the leopard his spots? Then may ye also do good, that are accustomed to do evil." If the Ethiopian has power to change his skin, or the leopard his spots, then the sinner has power to change his life in and of himself. But the thought is, that if these cannot change skin or spots of themselves, then no one can change himself from bad to good. The reason is obvious. It is somewhat on the principle that no man can lift himself over the fence by his boot-straps. We once saw a picture in natural philosophy of a man in a boat, with sail up, and bellows working in the stern of the craft, blowing on the sail. Now, the question arises, Why could

I Am Pure From My Sin. 53

not one lift himself over the fence with his bootstraps, or the boat be propelled by blowing on the sails? Simply because there is a back action in the whole business. When the power is exerted to accomplish the work there is a corresponding backward pressure which neutralizes the effort, and there is consequently a standstill. So it is in salvation. No man can save himself or make his own heart clean. There is a back action in it. There is a neutralizing force that brings things to a standstill. Here we see the utter failure of morality in saving the soul. Salvation comes from a power outside of self-effort. And yet one must put himself where that power can be exerted. We sometimes hear people say they believe in "working out their own salvation, with fear and trembling," as if salvation could be wrought out by any work on our part. How can one work out salvation when he has no salvation on hand? As well might Adam have tried to breathe in the Garden of Eden, before God put the breath of life in him. The one who expects to work out his salvation before God puts the salvation into him certainly has a very discouraging outlook before him. As well might a woman try to keep house without something to keep house on; or a grocer try to run a grocery store without any groceries on hand. There is altogether too much confidence placed in self-effort. If it were possible for one to save himself, why did Jesus Christ come into this world to save us? Did He come on a picnic excursion? Did He come just to show people how to live well? Was an example all that was necessary to save men, and could humanity do the rest? Is the vicarious atonement of Christ a humbug? Was there no danger of men going to an awful hell? Imagine one sitting high and dry on the beach, and another excitedly throwing him a life-preserver, and shouting, "Escape for your life!" If he did not think the man utterly crazy, he would at least think it was worthless and uncalled for interest he was taking in him. But, on the other hand, if that same person was out in the sea drowning, and some one should throw him a life-preserver, he certainly would not think it was out of place, but would quickly lay hold on it and be saved. The Savior did not look down on this old world and behold it high and dry, free from all danger; but saw a terrible wreck, and thus heaven's great Life-preserver came by, that all might lay hold on Him and be rescued from sin and hell.

Christ came into the world to do that which no man could do for himself. Some people turn over a new leaf, as if that would save them. Resolution is good, and no one can be saved without a resolution to live a better life; but all the resolution in the world will avail nothing in the way of salvation unless it brings one to Christ, who must do the saving. If one had the power to turn

I Am Pure From My Sin. 55

over a new leaf, and from that moment should never commit another sin, he would be lost just the same as if he had not resolved to do better. The explanation is this: Salvation does not consist in proper action simply from a given point in life till its close (even if that were possible). To the sinner it means not only right conduct, but it reaches both backward and forward. While the resolution is good, and ought to be made, yet there is a multitude of sins which he has committed in the past which must be settled and forgiven; and turning over his new leaf does not blot out the dark record. Thus, if one had power to live from this on without committing any more sin, he already has on him enough to sink him into hell. Suppose I go to the grocery store and purchase a bill of goods. I cannot pay cash for them, so obtain credit. My bill runs up to fifty dollars. I ponder it over in my mind, and come to the conclusion that I am not treating the grocer right. He has been very kind to me, and now it is time that I was turning over a new leaf. With a determined resolution to do the right thing from this on, I go to my grocer and tell him that I have not been treating him right; that I have turned over a new leaf, and from this on will pay cash for all I get. I purchase some more groceries, paying for them, and promising him that it will continue this way in the future. Now, this would certainly be better than the former method of running in debt, but what would the grocer think of my plan? While he certainly would be glad for the change in the program, yet he would no doubt think, if he did not ask, "What about the fifty dollars you owe me?" That resolution, you see, would not settle the back bill. Neither will the sinner's turning over a new leaf settle the past account with God. If he does not repent of the sins he has committed, and get forgiveness, he will certainly lose his soul in an awful hell. While one may pay his bill at a store, the debt he owes to God he cannot pay. He can only plead for mercy and say,

> "Jesus paid it all,
>   All the debt I owe;
> Sin had left a crimson stain,
>   He washed it white as snow."

God saw that man was utterly unable to settle the account, so Christ came into the world and bore our sins in His own body on the tree, and thus opened up a possible way for all to be saved. Yet this redemption of Christ will avail the sinner nothing except he lays claim to it and avails himself of this privilege. For illustration: I lose my horse, and it wanders out upon the commons; and, being found there, it gets shut up in the pound. My friend passes by and sees the horse and recognizes my property. He inquires how much it will cost to redeem it, and when told, immediately pays the price, and then notifies me of the fact, and tells me to come and get the horse. Suppose I pay no attention to the fact, spurn his kindness, and never claim my horse? Would his redemption of it avail me anything? Certainly not. When Christ saw this world shut up in sin He paid the redemptive price to set us free. This price was His own life. He shed His own precious blood. He has been notifying us all down the ages to come and claim our redemptive rights. If we will not, then His redemption will avail us nothing. When the Emancipation Proclamation was issued some years ago four millions of slaves accepted it and became free. Over eighteen hundred years ago Jesus Christ issued an emancipation proclamation, and thus offered freedom to every bond slave of the devil. Many have accepted, and many are accepting it, and liberty is theirs. If one chooses to remain in bondage and serve the devil and sin, the emancipation proclamation will profit him nothing.

The pardon of sin does not bring purity of heart. The text before us asks the question, "Who can say I have made my heart clean, I am pure from my sin?" A clean heart and purity from sin (inbred) certainly mean holiness. Can any one say truthfully, I have done this work myself? Who would have the egotistical impudence to fly in the face of God's word and declare that he had sanctified himself? A believer can no more sanctify his heart than a sinner can save his own soul. It is the blood in both cases that does the mighty work. If it were possible to accomplish the work of cleansing one's own self, why the statement, "the blood of Jesus Christ His Son cleanseth us from all sin"?

While it is utterly impossible to do this ourselves, yet the atonement of Christ is sufficient to reach "deeper down and farther back" in the soul than sin has gone. If it cannot do this, then it is at least a partial failure. But who dares say it is a failure? It has cleansed millions before, and can do the same again. We will risk its efficacy, depend upon its merits, and trust in its power. The heart must be cleansed in this world. There is no provision for it in the text. Death is not the agency. Death is the result of sin, and sin is the work of the devil. Jesus does not need to call on the devil or any of his works to help Him out in His work of sanctifying souls. Bozrah's mighty Conqueror is all sufficient. Let Him undertake the contract, and He will not make any failure.

Reader, let Christ make your heart clean and purify you from sin.

CHAPTER VIII.

THE SEVENTH CHAPTER OF ROMANS.

This is a wonderful rendezvous. People come from the North, from the South, from the East, and from the West and find in this chapter a common solace. It is a very fitting chapter. What wonderful comfort it gives to many to find out that Paul had just such a hard time as they. How often we hear the expression, "Well, my experience is a good deal like Paul's," and then quote the seventh chapter of Romans, or pervert some of his other writings, making them mean what he never intended them to mean. Only the other day a lady remarked to the writer, when trying to justify herself in not being sanctified, that her experience was a good deal like Paul's. We told her if it was like his she was all right. Another lady once said that her experience was in the seventh of Romans, and she never expected to get above Paul. We wonder what that grand old apostle of full salvation would say now to these professing Christians, who are wresting his teachings "unto their own destruction."

In this chapter, Paul makes use of the following expressions:

"But sin, that it might appear sin, working death in me by that which is good."

"But I am carnal, sold under sin."

"But what I hate, that do I."

"Now then it is no more I that do it, but sin that dwelleth in me."

"For the good that I would, I do not; but the evil which I would not, that I do."

"Now if I do that I would not, it is no more I that do it, but sin that dwelleth in me."

"I find then a law, that, when I would do good, evil is present with me."

"O wretched man that I am! who shall deliver me from the body of this death?"

Looking at this chapter, as we find it with these statements in it, we ask the question, Was this Paul's experience at the time he wrote this Scripture? Paul was a Christian from young manhood to old age, and this was written only a few years before his death. So, if it was his experience at the time of his writing it, then we may suppose it was his experience from first to last. The gist of the statements which he makes is this: Sin wrought death in him; he was carnal and sold under sin; what he hated he did, because sin dwelt in him. He did not do the good that he ought to have done, but did the evil which he ought not. There was a law of sin in him which caused him to do thus. He cried out in his misery, "O wretched man that I am!"

The Seventh Chapter of Romans. 61

We will compare these expressions with some of his other sayings, and see if there is harmony. Comparing Scripture with Scripture is a good method of interpretation. The Word, properly understood, does not contradict itself. If all those who claim that they do not believe in holiness would only take this into consideration it would marvelously help to clear away their doubts. Now for the comparisons.

"But sin, that it might appear sin, working death in me," etc. Compare this with Gal. 2:20: "And the life which I now live in the flesh, I live by the faith of the Son of God, who loved me, and gave Himself for me." This was some two years before he wrote the epistle to the Romans. He declares that he has life—spiritual life. How one can have life, and at the same time have spiritual death, is a mystery hard to solve.

"But I am carnal, sold under sin." Then see Rom. 8:2: "For the law of the Spirit of life in Christ Jesus hath made me free from the law of sin and death." If one is sold under sin, by what process of reasoning can one make out that he is free from the same? When, a few years ago, they sold a negro under slavery, was he at the same time free from slavery?

"But what I hate, that I do." He says it was because sin dwelt in him. This sin caused him to do evil when he wanted to do good. He discovered that it was a law in him, which he called the law of sin, which brought all this about, and consequently, evil was an ever present factor in his life. How does this compare with I Thess. 2:10: "Ye are witnesses, and God also, how holily and justly and unblameably we behaved ourselves among you that believe?" Notice also his dying testimony: "I have fought a good fight; I have finished my course; I have kept the faith." Does this look like doing the things he hated; that sin was constantly working in him; that there was a law which kept him from doing what he wanted to do?

"O wretched man that I am! who shall deliver me from the body of this death?" Did wretchedness mark the experience of Paul? Hear him: "Yet always rejoicing."—II Cor. 6:10. We understand how one would be miserable had he to drag around with him a "body of death," and continually to have his good motives thwarted by the evil which was ever present; but we fail to see how one at this same time could look up and say that he was always rejoicing. If he were to give both testimonies at the same time, we would certainly think he was mistaken in one of them. But, says one, "Paul did not give both these testimonies at the same time." Now, we are getting at the truth of the thing. If we make Paul say that both these were his experiences throughout his Christian life, we certainly make him irreconcilably contradict himself. To make him say that this "wretched" experience was his at the time at which he wrote the epistle to the Romans, will cause the same contradiction. Does he not say in the sixth chapter, that "Our old man is crucified with Him, that the body of sin might be destroyed, that henceforth we should not serve sin?" Does he not say, "For he that is dead is freed from sin?" Does he not say, "How shall we, that are dead to sin, live any longer therein?" Again he says, "That like as Christ was raised up from the dead by the glory of the Father, even so we also should walk in newness of life." "For sin shall not have dominion over you; for you are not under the law, but under grace." "For when ye were the servants of sin, ye were free from righteousness." "But now being made free from sin, and become servants to God, ye have your fruit unto holiness, and the end everlasting life." Here we have diametric opposition in experience to the seventh chapter, and this all occurs in the preceding chapter. In the seventh he says that he was sold under sin; that sin dwelt in him and held the mastery over him. In the sixth he declares that the body of sin is destroyed; that the proper Christian experience is freedom from sin; that we may have our fruit unto holiness. Probably not more than an hour or two at the most elapsed between writing the two opposites. Now, the candid seeker after light will honestly look for an explanation of this, and not seek a refuge in something that will not enable him to pass muster at the judgment day.

The fact is, that the seventh chapter of Romans is a great parenthesis, thrown in between the sixth and the eighth, no doubt for the benefit of the Jews, as he says at the beginning, "For I speak to them that know the law." He does it to show the weakness of human effort under the law to give a satisfactory experience, either in saving from sin or satisfying the soul. Whether he meant us to understand that it was his actual experience, trying to obey God under the law without grace, or that he uses the first person singular simply as an illustration of one's experience in that condition, is immaterial; the lesson is the same. In the fifth verse of this same chapter he says: "For when we were *in the flesh,* the motions of sin (sinful passions, R. V.) which were by the law, did work in our members to bring forth fruit unto death." In the eighth chapter and eighth verse he tells us, "They that are *in the flesh* (unregenerate state) cannot please God." Here we have an explanation to the whole chapter. Coupling these statements with the thirteenth verse, where he says that sin worked death in him, shows beyond any question of doubt that he is describing the case of one *"in the flesh"* under the law. Not that he was in the flesh at the time of that writing, for he says, as just quoted, "For when we *were* in the flesh," showing here past experience. Being

The Seventh Chapter of Romans. 65

in the flesh, he had the experience of death worked in him, and, of course, could not please God. So in that condition he found evil present with him; the things that he hated he did; he was a wretched man, and cries out for deliverance. But, says one, in describing the experience of this chapter, he makes use of the present tense, which shows that it is his experience at the time of writing. And we have just proved that he uses in the fifth verse the past tense, describing the same experience, which is conclusive evidence that he is referring to his past experience. To say the least, it is an offset to the present tense argument. Does Paul contradict himself? By no means. His purpose is to impress this solemn fact upon the readers. He is a wise writer, and a great scholar from a human point of view. But when inspired by the Holy Spirit, his wisdom cannot be questioned. We want to call attention to the place where he changes the tense, and why. In describing his past experience he gives in the thirteenth verse his closing reason for this awful condition. Now, having made it plain that sin was in him; that the law revealed things in a clearer light; and that human effort was inadequate to the occasion, he puts it down as an inevitable result that such a state would follow, and, simply to make it more forcible, he changes to the present tense in the fourteenth verse, and says, "I am carnal, sold under sin." That is, under the conditions above described in the chapter, "I am carnal, sold under sin." Then follows a vivid and impressive account of the distressed state of such a man. Do we not resort to the same method of employing the present tense for the purpose of emphasis? Perhaps the familiar rule of speech obtained in his day: "Habitual truths are in the present tense," increasing the force. Suppose I should take the same plan in describing my experience to a friend; would he misunderstand me and say it was my experience at time of writing? Let us see.

"My Dear Friend:

"I want to tell you a bit of my experience. There was a time in my life when I thought I was good enough. I was unawakened, and was living a good moral life. But under the preaching of the Word I saw my uncleanness and sinfulness. I was all right before the light shone upon my path, but when the light came my sinfulness was revealed, and I found myself in a state of death. I try again to do good, but I cannot. The things I hate I find myself doing. It is the sin that dwells in me that causes the whole trouble. I find myself in a sad condition. "O wretched man that I am!" Who shall bring about my deliverence? Thank God I have found the way; it is through Jesus Christ my Lord. There is therefore now no condemnation in my experience, for the Lord has taken it all away, and enables me to walk no more in the old sinful state."

The Seventh Chapter of Romans. 67

If I should write thus to a friend, would he misunderstand me and try to make it out that I am yet in a state of sin and living a miserable life? He certainly would not. Yet I have changed the tense, just as Paul did, in the very midst of describing the experience.

It would seem that any candid seeker after the truth would notice the remarkable and sudden change in the experience which Paul is describing, which immediately follows the statement, "O wretched man that I am! Who shall deliver me from the body of this death?" Now hear him: "I thank God through Jesus Christ our Lord." Here is the change; here is the deliverence. He gets out of the seventh chapter and into the eighth —just what every sin-tormented soul ought to do. With triumphant joy he declares in the first verse of the next chapter: "There is therefore now no condemnation to them which are in Christ Jesus, who walk not after the flesh, but after the Spirit." Not only does he clearly show that now he is, at this writing, enjoying the grace of God, having all the condemnation consequent upon a life of sin removed, but he also has the experience of full salvation or deliverance from inward sin. Hear him in the second verse: "For the law of the Spirit of life in Christ Jesus hath made me free from the law of sin and death." Not only was he at the time of that writing free from the condemnation of sin, but also from the inbred sin, which was the very root of all his troubles.

In this lesson which is before us we have four laws mentioned, namely: The law of sin and death, the law of God, the law of the mind, and the law of the Spirit. It is a common belief that all through this life there will be of necessity a warfare between the law of sin and these other laws; that in the economy of grace the three good laws can no more than keep the evil law in subjection, but cannot expel it, till later on at the hour and article of death the three will conquer and overcome the law of sin. But was this Paul's experience? No. It took only one of these laws to finish the law of sin, and that in this life. "The law of the Spirit of life in Christ Jesus hath made me free from the law of sin and death." Blessed deliverance! Wonderful freedom! Who would not seek for this grace, rather than pervert Paul's language and hide behind sin?

But I hear some say, that the seventh chapter of Romans was Paul's justified experience, prior to his sanctification. If I remember correctly, Paul had a powerful conversion. It certainly was up to the standard of that experience. Is that chapter a proper delineation of a regenerated life? Reader, was that your experience as a child of God? Were you sold under sin? Did sin slay you and work death in you? Did you do the things that you hated, and the things that you

The Seventh Chapter of Romans. 69

would do, did you not do? Did you cry, "O wretched man that I am?" We are confident that God's regenerating power produces a better life than this. We do not deny that there come times in the justified life, when one feels the workings of sin. We know this is true. One may have times when sin gets the upper hand and causes him to do the things that he hates. In fact, as he endeavors to keep up the spiritual life and finds such an evil principle within, he may in a discouraged moment cry out, "O wretched man that I am!" We do not deny the occasions, but we do deny that this is the *life*. Paul was giving this as his every-day life. This is not the life of a converted person. It is not the experience that Jesus gave me in conversion. I was not wretched. The Lord gave me power over the troublesome evil within. I found out that it was there, but had the blessed victory over it. I do not mean to say that I never yielded to its power, but that certainly was not my life.

I am well aware of the fact that this is a mooted question with many as to whether this was Paul's experience in justification or not. It was not my object to discuss this phase, but to show that it was not his experience at the time of writing the epistle. To show that we are not alone, however, in both views, we quote from Wesley's Notes on this seventh chapter of Romans. Beginning with the seventh verse, he says: " '*What* shall we say then?' This is a kind of digression (to the beginning of the next chapter), wherein the apostle, in order to show, in the most lively manner, the weakness and inefficiency of the law, changes the person, and speaks as of himself concerning the misery of one under the law. This, St. Paul frequently does when he is not speaking of his own person, but only assuming another character. (Rom. 3:6; I Cor. 10:30; chap. 4:6.) The character here assumed is that of a man first ignorant of the law, then under it, and sincerely but ineffectually striving to serve God. To speak thus of himself, or of any true believer, would be foreign to the whole scope of his discourse; nay, utterly contrary thereto, as well as to what is expressly asserted. (Chap. 8.2.) 'Is the law sin?' Sinful in itself, or a promoter of sin? 'I had not known lust.' That is, evil desire. I had not known it to be sin. Nay, perhaps I should not have known that any such desire was in me. It did not appear till it was stirred up by the prohibition."

We think that a few thoughts from Clarke's Commentary would help establish this truth upon the hearts of the people. Commenting upon this chapter in Romans, he says, concerning the fourteenth verse: *But I am carnal, sold under sin.* "This was probably, in the apostle's letter, the beginning of a new paragraph. I believe it is agreed, on all hands, that the apostle is here demonstrating the insufficiency of the law in opposition to the Gospel. That by the *former* is the *knowledge;* by the *latter,* the *cure of sin.* Therefore, by *I* here he cannot mean *himself,* nor any *Christian believer;* if the contrary could be proved the argument of the apostle would go to demonstrate the insufficiency of the *Gospel,* as well as the *law.*

"It is difficult to conceive how the opinioin could have crept into the church, or prevailed there, that 'the apostle speaks here of his *regenerate state;* and that what was, in such a state, true of himself, must be true of all others in the same state.' This opinion has most pitifully and most shamefully not only lowered the standard of Christianity, but destroyed its influence and disgraced its character. It requires but little knowledge of the spirit of the Gospel, and of the scope of this episitle, to see that the apostle is here either personating a Jew, under the law and without the Gospel, or showing what his own state was when he was deeply convinced that by the deeds of the law no man could be justified; and had not as yet heard those blessed words, *Brother Saul, the Lord Jesus that appeared unto thee in the way, hath sent me that thou mightest receive thy sight, and be filled with the Holy Ghost.—Acts 9:17.*

"In this and the following verses he states the contrariety between *himself* or any Jew while without Christ, and the *law* of God. Of the latter he says *it is spiritual;* of the former, *I am carnal, sold under sin.* Of the *carnal man,* in oppositioin to the *spiritual,* never was a more complete or accurate description given. * * *

"Those who are of another opinion maintain that by the word *carnal* here the apostle meant that *corruption* which dwelt in him *after his conversion;* but this opinion is founded on a very great mistake, for, although there may be, after justification, the remains of the carnal mind, which will be less or more felt, till the soul is completely sanctified, yet the man is never dominated from the *inferior* principle, which is under control, but from the superior principle, which habitually prevails. * * *

"But the word *carnal,* though used by the apostle to signify a state of death and enmity against God, is not sufficient to denote all the evil of the state he is describing; hence he adds, *sold under sin.* This is one of the strongest expressions which the Spirit of God uses in Scripture to describe the full depravity of fallen man. * * *

"We must, therefore, understand the phrase, '*sold under sin,*' as implying that the soul was *employed in the drudgery of sin;* that it was *sold over* to this service, and had no power to disobey this tyrant until it was redeemed by another. And if a man be actually sold to another, and he acquiesce in the deed, then he becomes the legal property of that other person. This state of bond-

The Seventh Chapter of Romans. 73

age was well known to the Romans. The sale of slaves they saw daily, and could not misunderstand the emphatical sense of this expression. Sin is here represented as a *person;* and the apostle compares the dominion which sin has over the man in question, to that of a master over his legal slave. Universally through the Scriptures man is said to be in a state of bondage to sin, until the Son of God make him free; but in no part of the Sacred Writings is it ever said that the *children of God* are *sold under sin.* Christ came to deliver the lawful captive and take away the prey from the mighty. *Whom the Son maketh free, they are free indeed.* * * *

"I have been the more particular in ascertaining the genuine sense of this verse, because it determines the general scope of the whole passage."

We think that these deductions ought to be sufficient to prove to any candid seeker after truth that the seventh chapter of Romans is not a delineation of the apostle's experience at the time of that writing, or between his conversion and sanctification; but that of a sinner under the law, trying to be right and utterly failing, because lacking the grace of God.

Let me say in concluding this chapter, if the reader is still in the seventh of Romans, do as Paul did—leap over into the eighth with joyful triumph, and then testify to the blessed deliverance.

CHAPTER IX.

PAUL'S THORN IN THE FLESH.

In the second epistle to the Corinthians, twelfth chapter, is the record of Paul's "thorn in the flesh." This fact in the experience of the great apostle has caused a great deal of comment, and has been fearfully wrested and misunderstood. Among the different opinions extant concerning what it was, and certainly the least tenable, is the one which claims that it was the "old man;" or, in other words, inbred sin. A little careful study on this subject would no doubt satisfy any one as to what it was, how, when and where he received it. Certainly it can be shown that it was nothing in connection with sin.

In introducing the subject, he says: "I knew a man in Christ above fourteen years ago (whether in the body, I cannot tell; or whether out of the body, I cannot tell; God knoweth); such an one caught up to the third heaven. And I knew such a man (whether in the body, or out of the body, I cannot tell; God knoweth); how that He was caught up into Paradise, and heard unspeakable words, which it is not lawful (margin, possible) for a man to utter."

He then goes on to say: "And lest I should be

Paul's Thorn in the Flesh. 75

exalted above measure through the abundance of the revelations, there was given to me a thorn in the flesh, the messenger of Satan to buffet me, lest I should be exalted above measure."

As every one knows, the man of whom he speaks, that was caught up into the third heaven, was himself. In this state he had great revelations of the glories of the heavenly world. No doubt the apostle's meaning when he speaks of making known those revelations was that it was impossible, rather than unlawful, to do so. The first thing we wish to settle in this lesson is, that this thorn was not carnality.

1. He states that the thorn came in connection with those revelations. Then, if it came at the time of the revelations, he certainly did not have it before. If the thorn was carnality, he did not have carnality just before the heavenly revelations.

2. He said it was a thorn *in the flesh*. The word flesh in the Scriptures has two meanings—physical corporeity and carnality. In reference to the physical he says: "The life which I now live *in the flesh* I live by the faith of the Son of God." —Gal. 2:20. In reference to the carnal he says: "So they that are *in the flesh* cannot please God." —Rom. 8:8. Flesh in both of these expressions cannot mean the same, else it would be an irreconcilable contradiction. To which flesh did the apostle have reference in the expression, "thorn in the flesh"? To say that he meant carnality is non-

sense. It would be the same as saying he had carnality in carnality if the thorn in the flesh was such. Then it must have been something which happened to his physical being.

3. It was given him lest he "should be exalted above measure through the abundance of the revelations." In other words, it was given him to keep him humble. If the thorn in the flesh was inbred sin, then inbred sin was given him to keep him humble. But the very root of pride, which is the opposite of humility, is inbred sin. Strange that something which produces pride should be given him to prevent the same. If carnality keeps people humble, then unsanctified people are more humble than the sanctified, and the more carnality the better.

4. He prayed three times that it might be removed, but the Lord saw it to be best that it should remain. Now "the carnal mind is enmity against God; for it is not subject to the law of God, neither indeed can be."—Rom. 8:7. Strange that God would want something to remain in him that was not subject to His law, but was real enmity against Himself. Paul had written to the Romans about the time in which he had these revelations, and had declared that the "old man" was crucified, and that the body of sin was destroyed; so then he must have been free from it.

5. The best thing God could do then, consistent with His will, was to let the thorn remain, and to

say, "My grace is sufficient for thee." Is this the way that God deals with the question of carnality? This is the way some people deal with it. They think that we must battle against it all our life; that God's grace is sufficient for us; but that He will not destroy this element till we die. But the teaching of His Word throughout is, that we must have it destroyed now.

6. Paul, in the ninth verse, defines the thorn in the flesh, and names it "infirmities," showing that it was a combination of things rather than one in particular. Is there any Scripture that makes inbred sin synonymous with infirmities? We have never seen it.

7. He said he would glory in the infirmities, meaning the thorn in the flesh. The idea of Paul, after he had said so much in regard to getting rid of this awful fungus of the soul, turning around and saying, most gladly would he glory in it. This he does, if the thorn is carnality.

8. He had scarcely finished the sentence of glorying in it, till we hear him say he takes pleasure in the same. What! take pleasure in carnality? Just so, if the thorn in the flesh is such. Anyway, we may wonder how he could take pleasure in that which a little while before he was so anxious to be rid of. Here we have the blessed proof of God's abounding grace, which is not only sufficient to make us endure for Jesus' sake the trials of life, but will also enable us actually to take pleasure in them.

We think we have given sufficient proof that the thorn in the flesh was not carnality. What, then, was it? If it was not inbred sin, then it was something in connection with his physical body. He said it took place fourteen years previous. In the margin of the Oxford Bibles are these words: "A. D. 46. At Lystra, Acts 14:6." Turning to this fourteenth chapter of Acts, we find the account of Paul being stoned at Lystra, and dragged out of the city as a dead man. There is no doubt but that Paul was stoned to death at this time. Here he was caught up into Paradise, and saw and heard things that no mortal tongue could utter. What a change from the scenes of a moment before! With a howling mob around him, throwing brick-bats, and filling the air with their fiendish yells, it seems that he departs this life, and the next moment he finds himself amid the glories of the third heaven. God had a purpose in it all, of course, but was not ready for Paul to leave the toils of soul-saving down here. One might imagine the Lord saying, "Paul, what are you doing here? I am not quite ready for you to come home. There are some more souls for you to save down there, and you will have to spend a little more time in the work; then I will send for you." We think Paul, without any word of reluctance, said, "Amen," and while the waiting disciples were viewing his mangled remains, life came into the body again and Paul arose to his feet. Right here let me say that Paul evidently believed one could be absent from the body, and yet be in a state of consciousness. He was not a soul-sleeper.

We see little opportunity for doubt that Paul had direct reference to his stoning at Lystra, being the time that he had the revelations, and consequently at this time he received the thorn in the flesh. Then, what was the thorn? Just what any one would naturally suppose, viz., some physical affliction as a result of the stoning. We could hardly suppose that one could undergo such maltreatment, resulting in death (at least for a little time), without some disfigurement of the body. It would not take many blows upon the face to render it more or less shapeless throughout life, even if it did get well. There are some Scriptural evidences which show very conclusively that such was the case with Paul, and, having these things to contend with throughout the latter portion of his life, we may well suppose it occurred at the time of his stoning, and hence, was the thorn in his flesh.

Immediately after speaking of the thorn and praying for its removal, he breaks forth in these words: "Wherefore I take pleasure in weaknesses, in injuries, in necessities, in persecutions, in distresses, for Christ's sake, for when I am weak, then am I strong." (Rev. Ver.) It is evident that every word used here is in connection with this disagreeable thorn. First, through it he had weaknesses. Surely, there was some weakness as a result of that awful stoning. Second, he said he had injuries. Natural enough. Injuries that disfigured him, as we shall soon see. Then follows the word necessities. These were the natural result of his weaknesses and injuries. He was under the necessity of having certain care and help, which he otherwise no doubt would have dispensed with. Then he mentions persecutions. These persecutions came, no doubt, as a result of the thorn of which he speaks. Even some of the professed followers of the Lord brought about persecutions on account of his appearance. "For his letters, say they, are weighty and powerful; but his bodily presence is weak, and his speech contemptible."—II Cor. 10:10. Persecutions from the brethren are worse by far than from the world. Following persecutions, he speaks of distresses. It is reasonable to suppose that this affliction, the thorn in the flesh, was a constant mortification, in a sense, to him. The distressing fact of his facial appearance was continually confronting him.

But this is not the only evidence concerning the nature of the thorn. According to some statements he makes to the Galatian church, it leaves little room for doubt that his trouble was a mutilated condition of his face, particularly affecting his eyes. We do not mean to infer that he had sore eyes, but a scarred face and weakened eye sight, that made him appear unsightly. Hear him in his address to that church: "And my temptation, which was in my flesh, ye despised not, nor rejected; but received me as an angel of God, even as Christ Jesus."—Gal. 4:13. He seemed so thankful to them that they did not reject him on account of his physical condition. In the next verse he even feels that they would have been willing to make an exchange of what was complete in them for what was so afflicted in Paul. "For I bear you record, that, if it had been possible, ye would have *plucked out your own eyes*, and have given them to me." It seems quite conclusive that his trouble was mainly with his eyes. As a further proof of this, we would call attention to the fact that Paul almost constantly had a companion with him, probably not only as an amanuensis, but a helper, because of impaired eye sight. Probably the only epistle Paul wrote with his own hands was to these Galatians. Evidently the reason why he did not write more was his practical inability. He did write the letter to these Galatians, for they had drifted into a sad state spiritually, and Paul, to prove that it was his own epistle, wrote it with his own hand, so that it would carry with it as much weight as possible. In our Authorized Version he says, in the sixth chapter and eleventh verse: "Ye see how large a letter I have written unto you with mine own hand." But the Revised Version brings a further proof concerning the weakness of his eyes, when it says: "See how large letters I write unto you with mine own hand." This shows not only that he wrote the letter with his own hand, but that it was written in large characters. Why large letters? Because on account of impaired vision, he could do the work easier and better. Probably the only way he could write at all.

Again, a little later in this last chapter of Galatians, he calls attention to his disfigurement, and says: "I bear branded on my body the marks of Jesus."—Gal. 6:17 (Rev. Ver.). Stockmen brand their stock in order to prove their ownership. Surely Paul had the marks of Christ's ownership. The injuries he sustained, especially at Lystra, were most conclusive and lasting evidences of the fact of his loyalty and blessed relationship to our Lord Jesus Christ. He had inward evidences in his own heart that he was fully saved, and he not only manifested to the outward world the fact by a holy life, but he had the very brand stamped upon him; something which the world was not carrying.

We would not like to lay this lesson aside without calling attention briefly to a few helpful suggestions. We learn from Paul's experience here that God does not always answer our prayers with a "Yes." If we would get the most out of our praying we must be so submissive to God that we will be as willing that He should say "No" as "Yes." If He answered in the negative, He will place alongside of the refusal, "My grace is sufficient for thee." There should be a continual understanding between every soul and the Lord, that wherever a negative answer is best it should be given. Of course, it will be done anyway, but with that previous understanding it would save one from the disappointment. Another lesson we may learn is, that the very things we naturally dislike the most may be so changed when God reveals His will in them, that we may glory and take pleasure in them. To live in the praise life, where one can "rejoice evermore" and "in everything give thanks," is a lesson which many Christians have not yet learned. Yet, with His sufficient grace, one can so live above the trials, or, rather, in spite of them, that there will be constant victory and rejoicing. Like Paul in this experience, one may have much need to undergo severe trials, not only to keep him where he should be in grace, but also to bring him out into much larger fields of usefulness, and thus prove God's all-sufficient grace. There are heights and depths for all of us to reach, which we have not yet seen. If we are only true to God, He will be pleased in one way or other to bring us into these places of further grace and glory. If we have some thorn in the flesh, instead of allowing it to trouble us and hinder us in the work, let us look to God, as Paul did, and if the blessed Lord does not see best to remove it, then He certainly will give grace to endure it; and not only to endure, but actually to joy and rejoice in the midst of it.

CHAPTER X.

THE STATEMENTS OF JOB'S COMFORTERS.

"Shall mortal man be more just than God? Shall a man be more pure than his Maker?

"Behold, He put no trust in His servants; and His angels He charged with folly.

"How much less in them that dwell in houses of clay, whose foundation is in the dust, which are crushed before the moth."—Job 4:17-19.

"What is man that he should be clean? and he which is born of a woman, that he should be righteous?

"Behold, He putteth no trust in His saints; yea, the heavens are not clean in His sight.

"How much more abominable and filthy is man, which drinketh iniquity like water?"—Job 15:14-16.

"How then can man be justified with God? or how can he be clean that is born of woman?

"Behold, even to the moon, and it shineth not; yea, the stars are not pure in His sight.

"How much less man, that is a worm? and the son of man, that is a worm?"—Job 25:4-6.

One great mistake which many make in reading the Bible, especially in the hit-or-miss way of reading, is, not discerning three things: First, who is speaking or writing; second, to whom is the person speaking or writing; third, about what the person is speaking or writing.

In answering these questions in the above quotations, we have much light thrown upon the subject.

We say we believe the Bible from cover to cover. We say that the Bible is the word of God. This is true. The Bible is the true word of God. It is a true record; an inspired record. Whenever it records any circumstance we can rely upon its truthfulness, no matter whether it is the record of some good deed of a good person, or of a bad deed of some bad person; whether it is the record of some true statement of a true person, or a false statement from a false person. It is a faithful record of whatever it undertakes to tell. There are some statements in the Bible which are not true, because they are made by false people. The record of them, however, is true, but it is the record of somebody's false assertion. For example, notice this statement in I Kings 13:18: "He said unto him, I am a prophet also as thou art; and an angel spake unto me by the word of the Lord, saying, Bring him back with thee into thine house, that he may eat bread and drink water." Now, was this statement of the man true or false? Did an angel tell him that or not? If the angel did not tell him that, then he lied, and the Bible would be giving a true record of an untrue statement. Let us see if the man told the truth. In the very next line are these words: *"But he lied unto him."* He made a false statement, but the Bible gives a true record of said lie. Thus we see that all assertions in the Bible may not be true. It depends upon where the assertion comes from. Observe, then, the importance of keeping in mind the above mentioned three points.

We will now consider the statements in the three texts under consideration. The first two we notice, by the heading of the chapters, were spoken by Eliphaz, the Temanite, and the last by Bildad, the Shuhite. These were Job's comforters. "Miserable comforters are ye all," he adds, in the sixteenth chapter and second verse.

In the first text is the statement that God puts no trust in His servants, and charges His angels with folly; and then, basing his argument upon this premise, he puts Job at tremendous disadvantage. He confesses that he obtained his information from a spirit in a vision in the night. Evidently he had not tried the spirit whether it was of God (I John 4:1), for the whole tenor of Scripture is, that He does put trust in His servants, and some day He will say, "Well done, thou good and faithful servant." That He charged His angels with folly we have never found in the record, unless it was Satan and his host, but that would be a strange structure upon which to base an argument against Job. or any one else.

The argument in the second text is, that He put no trust in His saints, and the heavens are not clean in His sight, sandwiching this in between two slurs concerning Job's piety.

Where Eliphaz got this information he does not say; perhaps that same spirit was still instructing him. At any rate, we fail to find any in inspiration to that effect. We cannot understand how the heavens can be unclean, when He made them. Why should He make unclean things or places? Heaven is His abode; does He dwell in an unclean place? We have always regarded heaven as a holy place. Is this not Bible truth? Can anything be holy, and yet unclean? Eliphaz, we believe your statements are far fetched; they will not stand the test.

We have the assertion in the third text that the moon does not shine, and the stars are not pure in His sight.

These are the words of Bildad, the Shuhite. He likewise slurs the possibility of man being clean. He seems to have copied it from Eliphaz, for the language is similar. We do not know where he got his information; possibly from the spirit that helped Eliphaz out. If he meant that the moon could not shine of itself, he was right; if he meant that no light came from the moon, he must have been blind. That the stars are not pure, we question his knowledge. God made them, and unless they are inhabited by sinners, we cannot understand how they can be impure. Bildad, our judgment is that you are worse "off" than Job, whom you are trying to make out such a hard case.

We would not feel so free to criticise these "comforters" if we did not have positive proof of the fact that they were worthy of criticism.

God said that Job was perfect, which is positive proof that he was not a liar; for a liar is certainly not a perfect man. Then, if he is perfect, and not a liar, we can well believe his testimony concerning these "miserable comforters."

What is your testimony, Job, concerning these men? Now hear him: "But ye are forgers of lies; ye are all physicians of no value." (Chapter 13:4.) They had been diagnosticating Job's case, and mankind in general, and, according to Job's statement, they had proved themselves very poor doctors. Hear him again: "How then comfort ye me in vain, seeing in your answers there remaineth falsehood." (Chapter 21:34.) Now, if Job told the truth, then certainly they did not at all times. They were trying to convince Job that he was not right with God; that his afflictions were a result of his sinfulness, and hence they were led evidently to use those extravagant expressions to sustain their argument.

But beyond the *prima facie* evidence of the falsity of the statements of these "comforters," and the truth of Job's testimony concerning them, we have the plain word of God himself. Hear the word of the Lord:

"And it was so, that after the Lord had spoken these words unto Job, the Lord said unto Eliphaz the Temanite, My wrath is kindled against thee, and against thy two friends; for ye have not spoken of me the thing that is right, as my servant Job hath." (Chapter 42:7.) And again: "And my servant Job shall pray for you; for him will I accept; lest I deal with you after your folly, in that ye have not spoken of me the thing which is right, like my servant Job." (Chapter 42:8.) Methinks I see Job erect a mourners' bench on the spot, so they could literally humble themselves in the dust and ashes (where Job had been sitting in his afflictions). Mounting it like an old-time campmeeting exhorter, he calls for penitents, and then sings:

"Come ye sinners, poor and needy."

Eliphaz hangs his head; Bildad turns both eyes toward the end of his nose; Zophar looks askance. Another verse is sung:

"If you tarry till you're better,
You will never come at all."

This brings them to time, and one after another quietly and humbly bows in the ashes at the mourners' bench. Job leads in prayer; hearts are broken; tears of penitence flow; confession and restitution are made; God forgives, and so does Job, and the burden rolls away. The smiles of acceptance beam out through their tear-bedimmed eyes as they rise to give in their testimonies. Job shouts "Glory to God!" shakes their hands, and sings:

"Hallelujah, 'tis done," etc.,

And exhorts them not to stop, but "go on unto perfection," and not lay again "the foundation of repentance."

After bidding them a final farewell, we see them leaving for their respective districts, inwardly resolving to get up a district camp-meeting at once, and hoping to secure Evangelist Job to conduct the services.

Meanwhile the opening heavens are pouring upon Job a blessing he can scarcely contain. This is the record: "And the Lord turned the captivity of Job, when he prayed for his friends; also the Lord gave Job twice as much as he had before." (Chapter 42:10.)

What flocks of sheep, and herds of oxen, and droves of camels and asses! Sons and daughters are born unto him. Fairer daughters are not to be found in the land. Job lives an hundred and forty years more, and dandles the fourth generation on his knees. "So Job died, being old and full of years."

Many people do not understand Job. They are apt to take sides with those "comforters," and even with Satan. If these people who thus criticise him had to undergo the tithe of his suffering in the various ways in which he suffered, we fear they would not come through as Job said he would: "When He hath tried me I shall come forth as gold." (Chapter 23:10.) God was putting him through deeper experiences than he had ever gone through before. Though He said Job was perfect, yet there were heights and depths which he had not reached; experiences which he had not yet learned; a knowledge of himself which he had hitherto not known. All of this was brought about through suffering. In a word, he had his holiness perfected through suffering.

So there are in us, after we are sanctified, many things to get rid of; things to learn; deeper depths to be sounded. There are many things in us which are not sinful *per se*, but are not of God. So God has post-purity processses for us in the way of suffering in many ways to bring us more and more into the matured life of Christian manhood. "Perfecting holiness in the fear of God" will be our experience if we stand and endure.

"So the Lord blessed the latter end of Job more than the beginning." And thus will He do with the sanctified to-day if they will only let Him have His way.

CHAPTER XI.

THERE IS NONE GOOD BUT ONE.

"And behold, one came and said unto Him, Good Master, what good thing shall I do, that I may have eternal life?

"And He said unto him, Why callest thou me good? There is none good but one, that is, God; but if thou wilt enter into life, keep the commandments."—Matt. 19:16-17.

Isolate this text, take it exactly as it reads, and it furnishes a good refuge for those who are hunting for excuses for not being sanctified. Isolate another segment of the Word in the fourteenth Psalm, and we have the astounding statement, "There is no God." It is either suggestive of ignorance or maliciousness when one takes an isolated statement and teaches from it some doctrine contrary to the general tenor of the Scriptures.

"The Bible, its own commentary," is certainly a suggestion worthy of all our attention. Comparing Scripture with Scripture will frequently solve very hard spiritual problems and unlock great mysteries. Following this course in the present case, we shall see the thought that was in the mind of the Savior. Do the Scriptures teach goodness as a moral quality in any one but God? If they do, then we are shut

There is None Good but One. 93

up to one of two things: either the Bible contradicts itself, or else the text under consideration does not mean what some opposers of holiness claim that it means. Let us compare it with some other Bible statements:

"And behold, there was a man named Joseph, a counsellor, and he was a *good* man, and a just."—Luke 23:50. If there were none good but one, how then could Joseph be a good man?

"For he (Barnabas) was a *good* man, and full of the Holy Ghost and of faith."—Acts 11:24. Where is the reconciliation with this text, if only one is good?

"For men shall be lovers of their own selves, * * * despisers of those that are *good*."—II Tim. 3:2-3. If there were no good people, how could any one despise those that are good? Can one despise a nonentity?

"For a bishop must be * * * a lover of hospitality, a lover of *good* men, sober, just, holy, temperate."—Titus 1:7-8. If there were no such a thing as good men, why did God require love for such? Would God ask one to love something or some persons not existing?

Perhaps we have given enough texts to show the true teachings of the Scriptures in this regard.

We come back to our former text and seek for reconciliation with these others. "There is none good but one, that is, God." We have already written a chapter on "There is none righteous, no, not one," and have shown that in the natural or unregenerate state there is none righteous; and with the same method of proof we would see that there is none good in his unregenerate state. David informed us in the fifty-first Psalm that he was shapen in iniquity and conceived in sin. He was not the exception, but the rule. He has no reference to some sin on the part of his mother at that time, or that she was counted a bad woman, as some suppose, for the declaration is made in another place that she was God's handmaid. He simply made use of an expression that shows that depravity has been rolling down the ages, and every one that comes into the world is tainted with it. The mighty stream has been coming on since our first parents, and neither David found, nor have the rest of us found, any exemption from it. We were born into this world neither good nor bad. The tendency or bias toward sin was in us, but we were not sinners. No one is a sinner till he sins. An infant cannot sin, for it knows neither good nor bad. "Where there is no law there is no transgression." Sinfully inclined, but not sinners. There are two erroneous ideas prevalent concerning the state of an infant—one is that its heart is pure, and the other is that it is a sinner. A little thought ought to convince any one that neither is correct. The manifestations of anger, self-will, pride, jealousy, etc., are *prima facie* evidence that the root of sin is in the heart, and this in time will lead it

There is None Good but One. 95

into actual sin when the knowledge of sin becomes apparent. That it is not a sinner in its infancy we know, for God does not hold one guilty where there is no capability of knowledge. Sin must meet with its proper penalty, unless it is repented of and forgiven. But if a baby were a sinner it would of necessity have to remain such till it could understand repentance and pardon. Then, if it died before that time came, it would necessarily be lost, for sinners cannot go to heaven. So, all dying in infancy, would have no possibility of being saved. Thank God we have better knowledge of the future life of our precious babies!

Man, then, is born into this world without any moral quality of goodness. He will continue destitute of all goodness as long as he lives, and throughout eternity, unless he receives it from Him who alone has inherent goodness. God only has goodness, as a natural attribute of His being. There is no possibility of any one becoming good except as he derives it from God. It is beyond the power of human attainments, either by resolution or moral deeds, to make one's self good. There is none good but one, that is, God. When Paul testified to his sinful state as a Jew under the law, he said: "For I know that in me (that is, in my flesh) dwelleth no good thing."—Rom. 7:18. This was not only Paul's experience, but that of all of us in our unregenerate state. The sooner the sinner wakes up to the fact that there is nothing in him that measures up to the Scripture standard of goodness, the better. The quality of goodness does not exist in him, and never will till he gets in union with Christ. We may speak in kindly terms of a friend, and say that he is a good man, or that he has a good heart, but the Word of God will not substantiate the statement unless he is a Christian. Goodness cannot be found apart from Him who is the Author of it. Just as there is, apart from Christ, no holy, righteous, Christian man, so there is, apart from Him, no good man.

Again, we may look at this text from another standpoint. The experience of perfection is taught in the Word, and numerous examples of it are mentioned; but perfection in the absolute belongs only to God. While all should measure up to Christian perfection, no one will ever be absolutely perfect. So it is with goodness. The way has been provided for all to be good, but absolute goodness will never be enjoyed by any human being here. Thus, if Christ meant there was no one good in the absolute sense but God, there is no apparent contradiction or mystery. So, in either sense, if we say there is none good in his natural state, or none absolutely good even in grace, the statement is harmonious with the rest of the Scriptures.

Some would try to prove that Christ is not divine, because He uses the phrase under consideration. If there were none good but God, then, according to His own statement, some say, He was not God.

There is None Good but One.

Properly understood, He no doubt was trying to fasten the fact of His divinity upon the mind of that young man. The thought evidently is this: "You have called me good. God is the One who is good. Do you recognize me as divine?" He certainly did so recognize Him, or he would not have sought Him as the source of eternal life.

In concluding this chapter, we wonder if any who are hiding behind this passage of Scripture, as an excuse for not being holy, ever expose their inconsistency by referring to another as being a good man. Consistency would never use the expression in relation to mortal man. O, for a proper understanding and appreciation of the Holy Word!

CHAPTER XII.

OUR VILE BODY.

"For our conversation is in heaven; from whence also we look for the Savior, the Lord Jesus Christ;

"Who shall change our vile body, that it may be fashioned like unto His glorious body, according to the working whereby He is able even to subdue all things unto Himself."—Phil. 3:20-21.

Some professing Christians seem to have an idea that everything connected with them is vile; that they are covered with Christ's robe of righteousness outwardly, but inwardly everything is vile. Of course, to these this statement of Paul is like oil on a troubled sea.

The writer once read of a conversation between one of these professedly "vile creatures," covered over with Christ's robe of righteousness, and a brother of clearer conceptions of truth. The former was asked if he were a Christian, whereupon he replied in the affirmative, though adding that he was a great sinner, sinning every day in word, thought and deed. He was then asked how he reconciled this with the Scriptures, quoting some passages relating to the mission of Christ on earth; what He was able and willing to do.

"Oh," he replied, "though I am a great sinner,

Our Vile Body. 99

yet I have Christ's robe of righteousness, which so completely covers me, that when God looks down upon me He sees nothing but Christ's robe of righteousness, whiter than snow."

"Indeed! Heaven is a holy place, is it not?"

"Yes."

"And there is nothing unholy that ever gets into heaven, is there?"

"No."

"And there is nothing holy about you except Christ's robe of righteousness, which covers you?"

"Nothing."

"Then when you come to die, what will happen? Christ's robe will pass through where it belongs, and you will pass on through where you belong."

Here we have irresistible logic, the Scripture verifying the same: "He which is filthy, let him be filthy still; * * * and he that is holy, let him be holy still."—Rev. 22:11.

We have in the text under consideration the following four thoughts: A vile body, the coming of the Lord, at which time the vile body will be changed, and that it will be fashioned like unto Christ's glorious body.

Many who oppose holiness are bolstering themselves up in the awful delusion that they will have to wait until the coming of the Lord or death to receive the necessary change which will qualify them for heaven.

Notice that this statement concerns the body

only, and not the soul. But the preparation is one of soul, and not of the body. When Jesus comes the change will be only in the body, and not in the soul. Neither death nor Christ's coming will make any change in the spiritual nature of man. All that change must take place here in this life, and that by faith.

That one who claims that we cannot be purified till death inevitably shuts himself up to the old delusion that depravity, or sin, is located in the physical, and not the spiritual, being. Is sin located in the corporeal nature? Let us see. Yonder is a limb which has just been amputated. The one losing it is lying there on the table. Would you judge there was any sin in that limb? I think I hear the answer, No. But suppose that both the lower and upper limbs had been amputated, and the patient was lying there on the operating table. Would there be any depravity or inbred sin in those limbs? Again I hear, No. But that poor man had sin in him before he went on to that operating table, and where is it now? Do I hear you say it is somewhere outside of his limbs, it must be in himself somewhere? But wait a minute. He does not rally from the operation, but dies. There is the dead body before you. Please tell me if there is any sin in it. Does that lifeless body, without feeling, thought, will, desire or knowledge have any sin in it? Who would be so foolish as to say, Yes? But a few minutes before, in that same body somewhere, was sin. Where is it now? Inbred sin is in the heart, in the inner being ,and not in the physical. Death makes a change only in the physical. It is the separation of the spiritual from the physical. If sin is located in the physical, then may we hope for purification or separation from sin in death; but it being located not in the physical, but in the heart, then nothing in death can effect the change.

Just so in the coming of the Lord. Those that are purified and ready for His coming will be caught up to meet Him in the air, and those that are not purified will not be ready. In this present evil world is the place to get ready for the world to come. The power of Jesus Christ and the efficacy of the cleansing blood are sufficient to purify us in this life without His need of calling upon "our last enemy," death, to come and help Him out. Praise the Lord for His all-sufficiency!

Let us come back to the word "vile" in its relation to our body and the coming of the Lord. At Christ's coming the mortal will put on immortality, and this corruptible will put on incorruption. The change, then, as we have before noticed, will be physical, and not spiritual. The words "vile body" cannot mean a body full of passion, and pride, and lust, and wickedness in general, for then one would not be prepared at all for the Lord's coming. We have the solution of the whole matter in the Revised Version, which reads, "the body of our humiliation." In this world we find evil on every hand. Sickness and sin and death surround us. Our bodies are subject to decay. We are frail creatures. We occupy a very humble sphere in comparison with that hereafter. So, Paul, considering all this, calls it "the body of our humiliation," and has no thought or reference to depravity whatever.

In view of that great day of days, ought we not to be ready? Jesus is surely coming. He is coming for those who are watching for Him and are ready for Him. Heaven's mighty magnet will sweep by this way some day, and who will be ready to rise? If a powerful magnet were drawn through a box of tacks, some of which were steel and some brass, the steel ones would adhere to the magnet, while the others would be left behind. Why would the steel tacks be taken up? Because they are of the same nature, and have an affinity with the magnet. Why would not the brass tacks cling to it? Because there is no affinity between them and the magnet; and again, there is too much of a composition there. So it is in our relation to Christ. When He comes, those that have the divine nature, and have existing between them and Christ the necessary affinity, will be drawn to Him and be forever with the Lord; while those who have a composition of the world, the flesh and the devil, and have no affinity with Him, will, of absolute necessity, be left behind.

Are we ready for His coming? Are we living

the kind of life we would like to be living when He comes? We should do nothing we would not want to be doing when He comes. We should say nothing that we would not want to be saying when He comes. We should go nowhere we would not want to be found when He comes. Surely He will come. The inevitable is before us. What shall we do? We should draw the lines just as close in our daily living as we would if we knew He was coming this moment. Dear reader, if you knew He was at the door, would you be ready with your present experience, without any further preparation? Or would you feel like begging Him to delay long enough for you to get ready? In an hour when you think not the Son of Man will come.

CHAPTER XIII.

I DIE DAILY.
I Cor. 15:31.

How often have we heard those who believe in a gradual process of sanctification quote this text to prove their argument! They do not believe that one may become dead indeed unto sin as a finality, and thus have carnality killed. But, on the contrary, they think they must die more and more unto sin until finally the "least and last remains of sin," by a process of daily dying, have become exterminated, just when they come to "shuffle off this mortal coil." We have known others, who are in the experience of holiness, quote this text to prove further processses of dying out after one is sanctified. We do not assume that there are not deeper experiences after we are sanctified, for we believe there are blessed post-purity processes in which we are further crucified or tested, and thus are enabled to go down deeper into the deep things of God than we at first comprehended in our sanctification. There are things that we did not see when we first died out and consecrated our all to God, although we subscribed to the whole will of God, and gave Him all we knew, and all we did not know. He did not flash all the light on our souls at once, for He knew just how much we could stand. Later on, when He saw that we could bear it, testings of a deeper nature came, which put us deeper into the life hid with Christ in God. Paul helped to fill up the measure of Christ's sufferings. He went through awful crucifixions and deaths, as it were, in different kinds of sufferings, after his purification; but in no sense was it a dying out to sin, nor did it touch carnality, for that question had previously been settled in the baptism with the Holy Ghost. We do not teach that when one gets sanctified, he is to sail to heaven on "flowery beds of ease." The "way of holiness" is not always strewn with roses, even though it be crowned with victory. Victory implies a battle fought and won. In the great work of salvation and growth in grace, God has very wisely ordered a course of drill and suffering which may consist of many things, in order to further and perfect the work already begun. But the God of all grace, "who hath called us unto His eternal glory by Christ Jesus, after that ye have suffered awhile, make you perfect, stablish, strengthen, settle you."—I Pet. 5:10. Deeper deaths do not imply a failure in the former one, or its insufficiency. It was all that God required and that could be done. It accomplished the work intended for it to accomplish. It resulted in the death of the "old man." But God wants us to grow in grace. He wants us to become stronger Christians. He proposes so to help us that the gates of hell shall not prevail against us. One way of accomplishing this needed growth is by processes of suffering and by revelations of our own further needs. We shall see things in ourselves that are not sinful, yet they are not the fruit of the Spirit. We die out to these, and more and more come under the direct control of the Spirit. Thank God for the grace that enables one to face the light as it comes, and stand all the suffering and bear all the trials subsequent to his purification. The one who thinks that sanctification is the point which precludes further growth in grace, and thus settles down, will soon find, to his regret, that he has made the mistake of his life.

While all of these further processes mentioned are true, yet nowhere do we find that the Scriptures teach a daily dying in order to get sanctified. Neither do they teach, that after one is sanctified, there is any further dying out to carnality. And especially does the text, "I die daily," have no reference to either thought. Then, what does Paul mean by the expression? We fall back on the common method and study the context. It means something, to be sure, and something that was daily occuring in the life of Paul. Let us notice the verse before and the one following:

"And why stand we in jeopardy every hour?

"I protest by your rejoicing, which I have in Christ Jesus our Lord, I die daily.

"If, after the manner of men, I have fought

with beasts at Ephesus, what advantageth it me if the dead rise not? Let us eat and drink; for tomorrow we die."

Thus we have it clearly set forth. Paul is stating that his life is in jeopardy every day and every hour. He does not know what moment he may be thrown in with wild beasts and be compelled to fight for his life. It would seem from the statements here that he actually had such a combat. He does not know at what moment some howling mob may pounce upon him and stone him to death. We know that he did have such an experience, for they stoned him to death, as they supposed, and dragged him out of the city. But God raised him up. Thus, we see, that instead of referring to a gradual process of purification by daily dying, or even further dying out subsequent to purification, he is simply calling attention to the fact of facing literal death daily. His physical life was in constant jeopardy. So the statement is one concerning physical death, and not of spiritual experience.

Reader, if you have not yet died out to sin, and had the old man crucified, do so at once. Go through the crucifixion now. Go on the cross, and let the nails be driven till carnality dies, so that there may come into your soul that blessed resurrection, "life more abundant." And if you are called to go down deeper, do not shrink nor waver, but constantly yield to the whole will of God, and let Him put you through any process He sees best. Thus, you will find yourself keeping saved, growing in grace, and becoming more and more rooted and grounded in Him. If, perchance, the persecutions of this world should reach the high-water mark of physical martyrdom, may we look to the God of Paul, who always caused him to triumph in Christ Jesus, Who gave him grace to say, as he faced the axman's block, "For I am now ready to be offered, and the time of my departure is at hand. I have fought a good fight; I have finished my course; I have kept the faith; henceforth there is laid up for me a crown of righteousness, which the Lord, the righteous Judge, shall give me at that day; and not to me only, but unto all them also that love His appearing."

CHAPTER XIV.

BE YE ANGRY AND SIN NOT.
Eph. 4:26.

How comforting this text is to some people! How soothing to those who have occasional spells of "righteous indignation"! How the devil helps them out in believing that their fit of anger was only righteous indignation, or nervousness, or weakness of the flesh, and so he whispers to them that they can be angry and sin not; that if they do have these spells, it is not sin, providing they always get over it before night, and never let the sun go down upon their wrath. O what a perversion of the Word of God! What a disappointment to the loving heart of Jesus when He wants to cleanse our hearts and save us from all our bad tempers, for us to bolster ourselves up under a delusion of the devil and perverted Scripture, and frequently give way to fits of temper, and then persuade ourselves that it is justifiable, righteous indignation!

We are well aware of the fact that we are flying in the face of the common opinion of Christians when we say that the text means just the opposite of what is generally supposed. We remember hearing one ask a minister what the text meant, whereupon he answered: "It is not the kind that beats the horse." We had often wondered what it really meant, and one day, when out alone in secret with the Lord, we came to this peculiar and generally misunderstood text, and, looking up to God, asked Him to reveal the real meaning. Scarcely was the prayer made when there was flashed upon our mind, as a light from above, this thought: "It means, be not ye angry, lest ye commit sin." This was just the opposite of what we had previously heard, so we concluded that at the first opportunity we would consult a commentary. On opening Clarke's Commentary we found that he had the same thought, which reads: "Perhaps the sense is: Take heed that ye be not angry, lest ye sin; for it would be very difficult even for an apostle himself to be angry and not sin."

One great trouble with professing Christians is, they look upon sin with too great a degree of allowance; they do not consider it an awful thing to do wrong. To sin *just a little* does not, to them, amount to very much. They seem to work on the principle that they may sin a little through the day, and when night comes they can pray and get forgiveness of all at once. Right here is where one begins to backslide. He may succeed in getting the day's sin cleared one night, and the next, and possibly the next, but if he is not careful he will be too tired and sleepy some night, and will not pray through and get a clear sky. He may even, after this, get things cleared up, but the tendency will be to get careless, and perhaps let the praying go over till the next night; and the first thing he knows he will have a clouded sky right along, and will be losing his temper, murmuring, neglecting duty and other things, without any particular compunction of conscience. Thus, he has drifted into a backslidden state almost before he knows it, because he regarded it a light thing to do wrong.

No, brother, do not get angry; there is sin along that road; the trail of the serpent is in that path.

It is true that Christ was angry with a righteous indignation, which is explained by the expression "being grieved." But His anger was not the uprising of unholy emotions, or fretful passions, or carnal propensities, but because His great loving heart was grieved; and if we have the same feelings in our hearts we shall be justified in them. But that the text does not mean something in which we are justified, it adds a few lines below: "Let all anger be put away from you." This looks very much like a contradiction, if the other means that we are to get angry. The strange part of it is, that many claim they have a right to get angry, but they must be sure and get over it before sundown, and not let the sun go down upon their wrath. Now, if it is a good thing to get angry, and we are commanded to do thus, why would it be so awful to continue past sundown? No; the proper meaning evidently is, "Be not ye angry and commit sin;" or, in other words, "Be ye angry and sin, *not;*" putting the emphasis on the last word "not," thus making it a prohibition against anger, instead of a license for the same, or a command. If, in the perplexities of one's environment, he should find himself overtaken with anger, he should overcome it at once, and not let the sun go down upon his wrath, thus using the words "wrath" and "anger" interchangeably. Christ proposes not only to enable one to keep in subjection a bad temper, but to eliminate it from the heart. Christ enthroned within will keep the heart in blessed equipoise in the annoying things of life, so that anger will not only fail to come to the surface, but will actually not exist. Blessed emancipation! Wonderful victory! Glorious experience! Who would not have it? O for the gentle Spirit of Jesus, that will enable us to suffer long, and yet be kind!

CHAPTER XV.

FORGIVE US OUR SINS.

"And forgive us our sins, for we also forgive every one that is indebted to us."—Luke 11:4.

"And forgive us our debts, as we forgive our debtors."—Matt 6:12.

Here we find, in the prayer which the Lord taught His disciples, a plea for pardon. Luke has it a prayer for the pardon of *sins,* while Matthew has it a prayer for the pardon of *debts.* To-day we frequently hear it, "forgive us our trepasses," which does not occur in any of the Gospels, although in Matthew it says, "But if ye forgive not men their trespasses, neither will your Father forgive your trespasses."

It has often been thrown at the professors of holiness that they have got beyond the Lord's Prayer. Also, it would seem to furnish a kind of refuge for those who believe that we cannot live above sin; for, if Christ taught His disciples to pray, "forgive us our sins," it would imply, as they suppose, that He expected them to sin every day, or there would be no need of the petition.

Speaking of the Lord's Prayer, we would say that no one is spiritually qualified to pray it unless he is sanctified or is seeking the grace. The first two petitions of the prayer say, "Thy kingdom come. Thy will be done." How much of His will does that mean? What is His will? A part of it is this: "This is the will of God, even your sanctification."—I Thess. 4:3. To pray for the Lord's will to be done, and then to reject sanctification, would certainly disqualify one for praying the Lord's Prayer.

But here is the petition for pardon in the prayer: In one place it says "sins," and in the other "debts." Of course, we understand that it does not mean the debts of a business nature, which are sometimes contracted between different parties. We should not expect to be forgiven them, but, like any honest person, go and pay them. It would seem that the words "sins" and "debts" are used here interchangeably. In the old order of things, there was instituted a Year of Jubilee. In that year, among the many blessings which came to those in trouble, was the cancellation of all debt. This certainly was hailed with much delight by those who were thus embarrassed. It did not work any hardship on the creditors, for when the obligations were made it was with the understanding that they were to be cancelled at the Year of Jubilee. Isaiah took up that year, with its many material blessings, and, in the sixty-first chapter, threw it into spiritual prophecy. Thus, as he looked down through the vista of time, he saw a day coming which was the great antitype of the old Year of Jubilee. The earthly blessings which came with that year, Isaiah saw were to be spiritualized. What they enjoyed in a material sense, the coming generations were to enjoy in a spiritual sense. Let us see when it was fulfilled. In the fourth chapter of Luke it is recorded that Jesus went into a synagogue and opened to this very chapter of Isaiah and read, among other things, concerning this Year of Jubilee. When He had finished, He said: "This day is this Scripture fulfilled in your ears." So, we see that Jesus brought in the great spiritual benefits, while the ancient Jews knew more particularly of the material. They forgave debts of a literal character; Jesus forgives debts of a spiritual nature. By coming unto Him, He will wipe them all out, to remember them no more against us forever. Debt places one under obligation to another. Every actual known sin, every mistake, indeed everything that will not measure up to the standard of absolutely perfect conduct, is reckoned as debt on our part towards God. Failure in any way to meet the perfect law of God and His will toward us throws us just so much in debt. It matters not whether it be intentional, or is done in utter ignorance of His will, the debt is made just the same. But God has made a difference in His own estimate of sin on our part; between known sin and a sin of ignorance. His own great heart of love would make this not only possible, but really necessary. So, in the Old Testament, we learn of the known sin, which had to be dealt with in a certain way, and also of sins of ignorance, which were answered for in another manner. There is not a person under the blaze of Gospel light who cannot receive an experience of salvation from actual, known sin, so that he can say:

"I rise to walk in heaven's own light,
    Above the world and sin;
With heart made pure and garments white,
    And Christ enthroned within."

And there is not a Christian, even in the very highest experience, but will make mistakes and blunders, and commit what the Old Testament calls sins of ignorance. A known sin will bring the one who commits it under condemnation and guilt. Before he ever is free from its effects he will have to pray, "Forgive us our sins," or, more specifically, "my sins." And as every *mistake* puts one under so much obligation to God, yet without that sense of condemnation and guilt that *known sin* brings, he will need to pray likewise, "Forgive us our debts." It would be well in this sense to pray the prayer daily. But to say that our Lord expected us to commit known sin daily, and that the prayer was intended for a petition in such cases, would show on the very face of it that Christ admitted that He was not sufficient to save unto the uttermost; that His atonement did not reach far enough; that there was a power which was stronger than His in the world. But thank God this is not the case. "Greater is He that is in you, than he that is in the world." How thankful we ought to be that God has provided a way back to Himself, if we are overtaken in sin, and have severed our connection with Him! On the other hand, we should likewise be thankful that He has provided a way so that we are not set adrift for every mistake we make; but that we may pray the prayer before us, and know that He who gave us the prayer will answer it.

More particularly is it expected, that in this blessed Holy Ghost dispensation, with the Comforter abiding within, we shall have additional advantages over any of those prior to the day of Pentecost. Christ gave the disciples that prayer before they had received the baptism with the Holy Ghost. After He came and took up His abode in them, they seemed to be different people. No doubt there was need of frequent return to that prayer, with broken and contrite hearts for forgiveness, before they received the "power from on high," but with the grace of full salvation and the mighty power of Pentecost in their hearts, we know that their walk was on lines far different from what it was before. Perhaps it might be well to call attention more carefully to this fact. We will take a look at these disciples before and after Pentecost.

I.—BEFORE PENTECOST.

1. *Unbelief and hardness of heart.* "Afterward He appeared unto the eleven as they sat at meat, and upbraided them with their unbelief and hardness of heart, because they believed not them which had seen Him after He was risen."—Mark 16:14. They had the root of the matter in them. The carnal mind had not yet been destroyed, and so they had that element to contend with, which at this time manifested itself in unbelief and hardness of heart.

2. *Unholy aspirations.* "And James and John, the sons of Zebedee, came unto Him, saying, Master, we would that Thou shouldest do for us whatsoever we shall desire.

"And He said unto them, What would ye that I should do for you?

"They said unto Him, Grant unto us that we may sit, one on Thy right hand, and the other on Thy left hand, in Thy glory.

"But Jesus said unto them, Ye know not what ye ask."—Mark 10:35-37.

Here we have carnality manifested in another form. Ambition to be somebody. Some are troubled in this way nowadays. The remedy for this disease is to take a trip to the "upper room," and to wait there till the holy fire falls and consumes inbred sin.

3. *A spirit of revenge.* "And they did not receive Him, because His face was as though He would go to Jerusalem.

"And when His disciples, James and John, saw this, they said, Lord, wilt Thou that we command fire to come down from heaven and consume them, even as Elias did?

"But He turned, and rebuked them, and said, Ye know not what manner of spirit ye are of.

"For the Son of man is not come to destroy men's lives, but to save them."—Luke 9:53-56.

This is another manifestation of this carnal Vesuvius, which lies in every unsanctified believer, and is ready with any provocation to burst out with its unholy lava and actually spoil the vantage ground one has gained since the last reckoning up time.

4. *Desire for popularity.* "And He came to Capernaum; and being in the house, He asked them, What was it that ye disputed among yourselves by the way?

"But they held their peace; for by the way they had disputed among themselves, who should be the greatest."—Mark 9:33-34.

As long as the "old man" is in the house there is no telling how and when he may raise a fuss. The idea of the followers of the meek and lowly Jesus striving and contending about human greatness! Yet carnality assumes some strange forms.

5. *Bigotry.* "Then Peter took Him, and began to rebuke Him, saying, Be it far from Thee, Lord; this shall not be unto Thee.

"But He turned, and said unto Peter, Get thee behind me, Satan; thou art an offence unto me;

for thou savorest not the things that be of God, but those that be of men."—Matt. 16:22-23.

Christ did not want to be defended, and especially not with human strength and weapons. Peter evidently thought he could successfully protect the Savior. The big perpendicular pronoun clamors for recognition if the "old man" is allowed to remain inside.

6. *Doubt.* "Except I shall see in His hands the print of the nails, and put my finger into the print of the nails, and thrust my hand into His side, I will not believe. * * *

"Then saith He to Thomas, Reach hither thy finger, and behold my hands; and reach hither thy hand, and thrust it into my side; and be not faithless, but believing."—John 20:25, 27.

Probably one of the worst troubles an unsanctified believer has with his heart is a tendency to unbelief. This awful thing is the blighting curse of the world to-day. The great remedy is a clean heart, full of pure love.

7. *Self-confidence.* "Peter answered and said unto Him, Though all men shall be offended because of Thee, yet will I never be offended.

"Jesus said unto him, Verily I say unto thee, that this night, before the cock crow, thou shalt deny me thrice.

"Peter said unto Him, Though I should die with Thee, yet I will not deny Thee. Likewise also said all the disciples."—Matt. 26:33-35.

We all know how sadly they failed in this. Self-confidence is one of the evidences of the presence of the "old man."

8. *Human dependence.* "Then Simon Peter, having a sword, drew it and smote the high priest's servant, and cut off his right ear."—John 18:10.

As long as carnality is in the heart it will seek to depend on the human instead of the divine. We never hear of Peter cutting off ears after Pentecost. He used another kind of sword for another purpose.

9. *Fear.* "Then all the disciples forsook Him, and fled."—Matt. 26:56.

This was the result of the inbeing of sin. Had they been filled with the Spirit they would never have forsaken Him and fled. Through fear, Peter even went so far as to backslide and deny the Master and curse and swear. But the Lord had mercy, and broke his heart and brought him back.

But we must do justice to these disciples. Some declare that they were not converted till the day of Pentecost. The writer was once stopped in the midst of his sermon by a Doctor of Divinity, declaring that he did not believe the disciples were converted till Pentecost. To take the ground that they were not converted till the day of Pentecost, is to fly in the face of Christ's own words concerning them. Let us see a few plain evidences that they were converted before the day of Pentecost:

1. *They belonged to Christ.* "Thine they were, and Thou gavest them me."—John 17:6.

2. *They kept God's word.* "They have kept Thy word."—John 17:6.

3. *They believed on the Lord Jesus Christ.* "They have believed that Thou didst send Me."—John 17:8.

4. *None of them were lost except Judas.* "While I was with them in the world, I kept them in Thy name; those that Thou gavest me have I kept, and none of them is lost, but the son of perdition; that the Scripture might be fulfilled."—John 17:12. If one is not lost, then he must be saved, for Jesus "came to seek and to save that which was lost."

5. *They were not of the world; had come out from it and suffered persecution for it.* "The world hath hated them, because they are not of the world, even as I am not of the world."—John 17:14. What a blessed thing it would be in these days if all who profess to be followers of the meek and lowly Jesus would so come out from the world, that the world would recognize the fact, and thus form a clear line of demarkation!

All of these clear evidences Jesus mentioned to the Father in His prayer for the disciples, and immediately prayed, "Sanctify them through Thy truth; Thy word is truth."—John 17:17. Showing conclusively that sanctification is subsequent to a clear case of justification.

Not only did they possess the evidences mentioned in Jesus' prayer, but we notice also that

6. *They had left all and had become followers of Jesus.* "Then Peter said, Lo, we have left all, and followed Thee."—Luke 18:28.

7. *They had marvelous power to cast out devils and heal the sick.* "And when He had called unto Him His twelve disciples, He gave them power against unclean spirits, to cast them out, and to heal all manner of sickness and all manner of disease.

"And as ye go, preach, saying, The kingdom of heaven is at hand.

"Heal the sick, cleanse the lepers, raise the dead, cast out devils; freely ye have received, freely give."—Matt. 10:1, 7, 8.

Suppose that one who manifests the spirit of a humble Christian to-day should be found doing such work, would not people think him a genuine Christian?

8. *Their names were written in heaven.* "Rejoice, because your names are written in heaven."—Luke 10:20. It is true that this had reference to the seventy that Christ sent out, but who would suppose that they had their names written in heaven and the disciples had not?

When we look at these disciples from the carnal side of their experience, and see sometimes the unbelief and hardness of heart, unholy aspirations, a spirit of revenge, desire for popularity, bigotry, doubt, self-confidence, human dependence and fear; when we see these things cropping out in them, we are constrained to cry out that they did not have any part or lot in the blessing of salvation. If that be the case, then the prayer, "Forgive us our sins," would certainly be very appropriate. On the other hand, when we look at the grace side of their lives apart from the carnal, and see that they belonged to Christ, kept His word, believed on Him, were not lost, were not of the world, were persecuted for righteousness' sake, had left all and were following Jesus, had such marvelous power, and that their names were written in heaven; when we see these characteristics, we are constrained to say that they were perfect. We wonder if the preachers who claim that these were not converted till Pentecost would refuse any one the privilege of church membership who had as good, but no better, experience than these? Or, should one of their members, with a like experience, die, would they not preach him into heaven?

The fact of the matter is, these disciples were very much like justified people to-day—there was a carnal side and a spiritual side in their experience. Sometimes they had the victory, and sometimes they did not. Sometimes they were up, and sometimes they were down. It was a sort of in and out, to and fro, time with them. It was a case of sinning and repenting. It was not all sinning, nor all repenting, but occasionally the "old man," which remained in the heart of these, as well as the "old man" which remains to-day in the heart of all

Christians after regeneration, would spring up and cause them trouble. But look at them after the prayer of Jesus for their sanctification was answered on the day of Pentecost. What a change has come over them and in them! The fire of the Holy Ghost has burned out inbred sin and purified their hearts. Now it is victory all the time. Instead of unbelief and hardness of heart, their hearts are melted down in the crucible of God's love and filled with the simple faith of Christ. Instead of unholy aspirations, and wanting pre-eminence and popularity, they are willing to take the lowest places. They are willing to be counted as the filth and offscouring of the world; they are willing to be banished and scourged and put in prison; anywhere with Jesus and anything for Jesus. Instead of wanting literal fire to come down and consume their adversaries, they would have the fire of the Holy Ghost come down and consume sin out of their hearts. Instead of the sword of steel to cut off the ear, Peter uses the sword of the Spirit and cuts into the heart. Instead of bigotry, and self-confidence, and human dependence, they have learned that they can accomplish nothing apart from Christ; that only in Him can they hope to succeed, and that in and of themselves they are nothing. Instead of all forsaking Him and fleeing away, they stand like pillars in the temple; they are ready to live or to die for Jesus; the prison is not too dark for them; the ultimatum of the Sanhedrin does not affright them; the blazing fagot only puts more fire into their souls; the glittering sword has lost its piercing terror; Patmos' lonely mount only brings the heavenly hallelujahs the nearer. Amidst howling mobs, and whirling brickbats, and ecclesiastical denunciations, and living deaths, the still small voice of Jesus is heard cheering them on the way. In the darkness of inner prisons the face of Jesus is seen smiling with approbation upon them. They are so filled with the divine presence, and so utterly abandoned to the Holy Ghost, that it makes no difference with them when they are killed or how they are killed. Instead of Peter denying his Lord, he constantly witnesses to His name; instead of cursing, he is found praising and shouting the constant victories of his Christ. Such was the power of Pentecost. O that to-day those who are opposing the full salvation of God, and bickering and caviling over holiness, would seek their Pentecost! Their hearts would rejoice, the church would put on new strength, and the world would be made better by their living in it. To your knees, ye critics, and pray, "Forgive us our sins."

CHAPTER XVI.

I KEEP UNDER MY BODY.

"But I keep under my body, and bring it into subjection, lest that by any means, when I have preached to others, I myself should be a castaway."
—I Cor. 9:27.

This is a great resort for holiness opposers. They summer and winter at this place. The harbor is full of them. They never get beyond Paul. O no! If he had to contend with the carnal mind, then they may not hope to be freed from the same in this life. Rather discouraging outlook, if this text means depravity in the heart.

We raise the question, What does Paul mean by keeping under his body and bringing it into subjection? Perhaps the Revised Version would throw a little light upon the subject. "But I buffet my body, and bring it into bondage." Does he have reference to the "old man," or simply the physical man? He certainly alludes to one or the other. One way, and a very good way, to find out the thought of a text is, to compare Scripture with Scripture. Let us try the plan here. Whatever Paul had reference to, he kept it under. Paul was on top. It seems that it required some attention, some effort to accomplish this, but he succeeded all right, and was an overcomer in the affair.

He tells us in Rom 6:6, "Knowing this, that our old man is crucified with him, that the body of sin might be destroyed, that henceforth we should not serve sin." Strange that he should be putting forth an effort to keep under something that was already crucified and destroyed. If the "old man" was crucified (death follows crucifixion), hence, dead, why should he need to "buffet" it, as the Revised Version has it? The idea of buffeting a poor corpse that could not lift its little finger to strike! Paul putting forth an effort to keep on top of such a thing, crucified and put off, lest it should get him under! The idea is preposterous.

Again he says he brings it into subjection. It would appear from this that it minded him; that he was master in the affair. Is this the way the "carnal mind" acts? Hear Paul on that: "The carnal mind is enmity against God; for it is *not subject* to the law of God, neither indeed can be."—Rom. 8:7. This evil principle within is not something that is subjugated. If it would not mind the law of God, I reckon it would not mind the law of Paul. You can buffet it, sit on it, stand on it, and tell it to behave itself, and it will not mind. When you think you have it suppressed, it will suddenly arise and claim authority over the possessions. You may order it to leave the premises, but it claims to have been on hand as early as anybody, and "possession is nine points of the law." You may think sometimes that you have made it quiet, but it is only "playing 'possum" on you, and will poke up its head when you are sufficiently off guard. It can stand a good deal of mistreatment if it is only allowed to remain in the house. It is very fond of some things, such as flattery, and style, and worldly amusements. It likes the cold. Dead, cold formality is its delight. It is much afraid of fire. All sorts of ways and means have been used to manage it. It has been *re*pressed, *sup*pressed, *de*pressed, *com*pressed, but the only sure way is to *ex*press it.

As long as it is in the house there will be trouble. We are told to "make not provision for the flesh." The best Christian life does not come from the subjugation of this element of the soul. God has provided something better than keeping it under. The atonement of Christ is sufficient not only to neutralize it, but utterly to exterminate it. (Let me say right here, by way of explanation, that this sin element is not a substance, but a condition.) There is a great deal of so-called holiness these days, which allows the "old man" to remain in the home. The Holy Spirit is emphasized a great deal, and the Christ life beautifully portrayed, but carnality is not properly dealt with. Now, as long as this "old man" is allowed to remain, he will put up with a good deal of inconvenience; but when the fire of the Holy Ghost is turned on he has to get out. We may talk about the Spirit-filled life and the Comforter abiding within, but the fact is, He will not come to occupy a temple wherein He cannot have supreme rule. Our bodies are to be the temples of the Holy Ghost, and if this experience is ever enjoyed, then will the recipient have to submit to the process of sin-eradication. We should give God credit for wisdom in His dealings. In this case He would act somewhat like a dentist. I go to a dentist, and tell him I have a tooth for which I am concerned. There is a decayed spot in it, and I am afraid that I shall lose the tooth. I ask the doctor if he can fill the tooth with gold, and thus preserve it. Upon examination he assures me that there is no reason why I should lose the tooth; that he can fill it, and thus it will be preserved. I submit to the process of filling. The dentist begins to apply his drill, and in a little while it reaches the quick, and I throw up my hands, crying, "O dentist, I didn't ask you to take my head off! I only asked you to fill my tooth!" He smiles and says, "This is the way I do it. I am preparing the tooth for the filling. If I should place the gold on top of that decayed part it would not remain there nor preserve the tooth."

"But it hurts so!"

"Yes, I know it hurts, but it will pay you to endure the pain for a little while, for the benefit you will receive in the filling."

So it is in the filling with the Holy Spirit. It is no child's play to get the Holy Ghost. We need

Him to fill our souls and preserve our Christian experience. He assures us that He will do this for us if we will submit to the process. It means something more than just to sit down and quietly say, "Fill me now." Before the Holy Spirit will come to occupy a heart, He must have it in a state of entire abandonment to Himself; a full consecration to Him; crucified indeed unto the world. This is suffering the loss of all things; the dying out to everything but God. The nails are driven, and it hurts. Many come down from the cross and save themselves from the crucifixion, only to suffer the greater agony of a guilty conscience and failure of full salvation. It hurts for awhile in the crucifixion, the preparation for the reception of the Holy Ghost, but it pays to endure the suffering for a little season in making the entire consecration, for the joy of being filled with the Spirit. This entire abandonment to God is absolutely necessary as a requisite to holiness. Is the question asked, Why does God so require? For several reasons.

First, He wants people whom He can trust. He knows that when one has gone through the crucifixion which precedes the gift of the Holy Ghost, and has "suffered the loss of all things," He can trust that soul.

Second, He wants people who will appreciate the gift. Something received without any effort put forth is not appreciated as that is which costs something. The young man that falls heir to a large inheritance is quite likely to underestimate its worth, and if not careful will easily let it slip from him. But that person who has toiled for the fortune he has accumulated will recognize its value, and will be frugal in its use. So, if the Holy Spirit could be received without any consecration or effort on our part, He would not be properly appreciated, and would probably be found wanting in the soul under extreme pressure. We would not magnify self-effort, or be understood to say that this blessing comes by works, or that the Holy Spirit would not come by asking Him to do so; but we do mean that it becomes absolutely necessary to make such a complete consecration, in order to get into a place where one can believe for the baptism with the Holy Ghost. Consecration clears away the rubbish, so faith can have a chance to make connection.

Third, when one has gone through the ordeal of this crucifixion in order to receive Him, he will be more apt to retain the experience, feeling that he would not like to go through that suffering again.

Fourth, the spiritual law of impenetrability obtains here: no two bodies can occupy the same space at one and the same time. The Holy Spirit will not occupy the heart in which the "old man" lives. He must be crucified and cast out. The full and complete abandonment of the soul puts one where this can be done, and the Holy Spirit will have no rival in the heart.

Thus, we see the theory, that one may have the

gift of the Holy Spirit, and at the same time have carnality in the heart, is a snare of the devil, and is deceiving many good people.

We come back to the thought of Paul keeping his body under. What did he mean? He meant just what he said—he kept his *body* under. It was not the body of sin, for that was destroyed (Rom. 6:6); but the corporeal body, with its natural passions, desires and members. Man is a trinity in himself—tripartite. He has a spirit, soul and body. Paul uses the expression, "And I pray God your whole spirit and soul and body be preserved blameless unto the coming of our Lord Jesus Christ." (I Thess. 5:23.) Notice that this follows that remarkable sentence, "And the very God of peace sanctify you wholly." From this we see plainly that we are first to be sanctified wholly, and then have our spirit, soul and body preserved blameless. This blamelessness is to follow the experience of entire sanctification. Three things are to be preserved blameless: spirit, soul and body. We further see that one may not be blameless in his spirit, or his soul, or his body. Outside the saving grace of God, one's spirit nature, his soul nature, and his physical nature are defiled. Paul made that plain in his letter to the Corinthians: "Having therefore these promises, dearly beloved (not sinners), let us cleanse ourselves from all filthiness of the flesh and spirit, perfecting holiness in the fear of God." (IICor. 7:1.) There are certain attributes which belong to the spirit, others to the soul, and yet others to the body; attributes which are not wrong, but pure and good, so long as kept in their proper place; so long as they simply perform what they were created to perform. When they are allowed to step outside their bounds they become corrupted. Paul, in saying that he kept under his body, had no reference to either his spirit or psychic nature (which, of course, were in their proper sphere), but simply to the physical. The physical nature, with all its attributes, he was holding the mastery over. If he did not they would soon be over the banks, and he would be subject to his own passions. He would be under, and his physical appetites would have the mastery over him. As it is said, the body makes a good servant, but a hard master.

There are attributes which belong only to the body; among these are the desire for food, drink, sleep and sexual commerce. All these are proper. They are in every normal body. There is something physically wrong where any one of these is wanting. They are God-given, and so long as they are kept in their places and perform only that which God intended them to, then may one say with Paul, "I keep under my body." Suppose Paul did not watch his eating. He feels a desire to eat something, which he knows would be injurious to him, or perhaps superfluous. This would be allowing his appetite for food to get the mastery over him. There would be no sin in the appetite, only in its wrong indulgence. So with drink. We are persuaded there are many Christians who are not keeping under their body in this respect. They eat those things which they are conscious hurts them, and drink that which is an injury to their health. Suppose Paul allowed himself to take more time for sleeping than he should. This can grow on one till it will become abnormal. One will become sluggish and lazy. Then he could no longer say, "I am master over my body," but his body in this respect would be his master. Sexual desire is pure and right. In the degeneration of humanity it is abnormal with many, and every one should look to God for deliverance from its perversity wherever it is discovered. But God placed within man that desire, and when only used with the approbation of God it is holy and right. But O, the mastery that this desire gets over men! How the strong have been slain! How the graves have been filled with its victims!

Not only does keeping the body under have reference to the above named desires and attributes, but every member of the body should be so guarded that it is made to fill the place that our Creator intended it to fill. Each member should serve, and not be master. Paul tells us in Rom. 6:13: "Neither yield ye your members as instruments of unrighteousness unto sin; but yield yourselves unto God, as those that are alive from the dead, and your members as instruments of righteousness unto God." The only proper way to keep these members in their allotted place is to yield them entirely unto God, and trust Him to enable you to be the master over them. Paul had them under him. He had feet, but he did not allow his feet to carry him into any place where he would have to leave Jesus outside. He had hands, but with them he served the Lord, and did not use them in selfish interests, or in any way in which he could not glorify Christ. With his tongue he might have engaged in foolish talking, in evil speaking, in murmuring and complaining, in lying, swearing and tale-bearing; in fact, in a multitude of ways; but he had One in him Who gave him grace and power over this member, so that he could say he kept that portion of the body in subjection. With his eyes he could behold things which would not be pleasing to God for him to see; yet in keeping his body under it would involve the power over the eyes so that they would not look upon anything or person in any way that would be displeasing to Christ. He could hear with his ears, but he watched that part of his body, and would not yield to hearing anything that would mar his Christian character. The fact is, that Paul kept his body, with all that pertained to it, in its proper place. What a testimony! Would to God that all Christians could give such a testimony! It matters not what heredity may do for us; what weakness may have been transmitted; what abnormal appetites one is cursed with; the power of the atonement in the baptism with the Holy Ghost is sufficient to enable any one to "keep under" his body. How good God is to provide such a great salvation! In the work of sanctification a mighty destruction takes place, yet there is nothing taken away that is God-given and that He has any use for. No part of our human nature is destroyed. He does not spoil one's identity. He takes not away our will. He destroys selfishness, but leaves our self. The "old man" goes, and the "new man" takes full possession. In this wonderful, God-empowered state, one is enabled to "keep under" his body. If in our human frailty we discover any part of this nature endeavoring to get out of its proper place, like Paul, referring to the wrestlers and boxers, we simply are to lay it out and hold it down. To keep on top, so to speak, in all the workings of our body is a state which all Christians should covet. This is not only our glorious, blood-bought privilege, but also our bounden duty. Thus keeping our whole nature in its normal and Christ-approved sphere, we may hope to succeed in our Christian life, and after we have preached to others, not be castaways ourselves.

CHAPTER XVII.

BE NOT RIGHTEOUS OVER MUCH.

"Be not righteous over much; neither make thyself over wise; why shouldest thou destroy thyself."—*Eccl. 7:16.*

It would seem at the first glance at this text that Solomon was swinging the danger signal, and warning the saints against being too righteous. Whether the king meant to do this or not, he has not wanted help to keep it swinging on down the ages. In fact, it seems to be the delight of some to stand upon the walls of Zion (?) and keep up the warning, lest people indulge too profusely at the well of salvation. If righteousness be a dangerous element in the soul; if the well of water springing up into everlasting life can be partaken of too freely; if holiness and death, as some seem to think, are inseparable; if an overdose of the elixir of eternal life is possible, and may prove a poison to the patient; if all this be true, then may some conscientiously feel themselves delegated with authority to watch careless partakers of the divine nature, and warn them of the danger of over indulgence. But if righteousness, either in small or large quantities, works no harm; if the more of the divine nature one has the better; if the stream of holiness passing through the soul leaves no deadly poison and is separable from death; then we see no reason for danger signals, or warning voices, or feelings of alarm. We ask, then, the question, "Is it possible to be over much righteous?" Are there any examples of such in the Bible? If so, in what respect were they over righteous? Will the alarmist please look up the records and note a few of these examples before he scares any more of the sheep from the water of life?

What about people in these days? Are there now any who are righteous over much? We think we hear the answer, "Yes." Then in what respect? Do you say, "Some will not ride on the street car, nor black their shoes, nor take milk from the dairy, nor bread from the baker, nor go to the postoffice on Sunday, and a score of other little things which other Christians do?" Now, to the law and to the testimony. Is there anything in the Word of God that condemns such people in these things, and proves that such conduct is over much righteousness? Do you say, "Some carefully abstain from wearing any gold upon their person, even to a wedding ring upon their finger; birds' feathers are an unknown quantity upon their hats; their dress is so very plain; they think they must be so careful in their eating; they never drink tea nor coffee, and swine's flesh never comes into their mouth"? All this indictment must be weighed by the Word of God, and these actions or omissions must be properly proved to be wrong, or these clients must not be convicted. In candid thought, is there anything in Scripture, either in the Old or New Testament, which declares that it is wrong to follow a course of action as described? If not, then it is simply prejudice that says it is righteousness in over abundance. But I hear another say, "Some people are all the time talking about their religion, and saying the Lord has sanctified them, and they bother other people about not having what they have, and it makes me feel uncomfortable. *They* are over much righteous." Search the Scriptures, and anything that the Word condemns we will judge accordingly; but until then we will have to decide that their righteousness is within bounds.

We have noticed this in the Word, that wherever there is a warning thrown out there are also examples of those who did not heed the signal. Now, as some would claim, here is a warning against too much righteousness; but where are the examples of heedlessness, either in the record of the Word or in modern times? Where is the person that the Lord would pronounce too good? Where is the one that has done too nearly right? Where is the one that has been too faithful and lived too close to the commands of God? Perhaps some one is saying, "It does not mean that one can be too good or too upright, but it means self-righteousness." One has no more right to say that

Be Not Righteous Over Much. 141

text means self-righteousness than that it means any other abominable thing. Self-righteousness is an abomination, and is nothing but "filthy rags." Any of it is too much, and the text implies that whatever the thing in question is, some would be well enough, but too much would not be good.

One of the largest religious newspapers in the United States has a page devoted to questions and answers. These questions are submitted to the people for answers, and the parties whose answers are chosen are paid for the same. In a recent issue of this paper appeared the following question, with its answer:

"What is the meaning of Ecclesiastes 7:16: 'Be not righteous over much; neither make thyself over wise; why shouldest thou destroy thyself?'"

Answer: "This verse may be taken as a caution against a Pharisaical display of righteousness, which, while wonderfully scrupulous about the letter, too often loses sight of the spirit of God's command."

Probably many other answers to this question came in, but this was chosen as the best. It is evident that the writer was not clear in his understanding of the text, at least he was not sure, for he states, "This verse may be taken," etc., showing that while it may mean something else, yet it "may be taken" in the sense given.

Of course, the Lord does not want anybody to do as this answer indicates, but that the text does not mean anything of the kind will appear when a proper study of the context is made. We believe it is right here that so much misunderstanding of the Word comes in. A passage of Scripture, as it stands alone, seems to teach one thing, and when used with its context means quite another. It means something, or it would not be there. God has not allowed meaningless words to come into His Book. Following the method of studying the context, we can see perhaps what the thought is. In the previous verse Solomon says: "All things have I seen in the days of my vanity." That is, in the days before he knew the Lord. In his natural, unsaved state, he observed some things. One thing was, he was watching the difference between the righteous and the wicked; the earthly prosperity and adversity of each. And, like the unsaved today, he was looking at things from an entirely wrong standpoint. This evidently is his thought when he refers to seeing things in his vanity. Then he goes on to mention some things which he had observed from that point of vision and at that time. He says: "There is a just man that perisheth in his righteousness, and there is a wicked man that prolongeth his life in his wickedness." This evidently was a temptation to him, just as it was to his father David, when he saw the wicked spreading themselves like green bay trees. David said:

"For I was envious at the foolish, when I saw the prosperity of the wicked.

"For there are no bands in their death; but their strength is firm.

"They are not in trouble as other men; neither are they plagued like other men."—Psalm 73:3-5.

He further said: "They have more than heart could wish." But he moved around to another location and looked at them from another standpoint, and said: "When I thought to know this, it was too painful for me; until I went into the sanctuary of God, then understood I their end." When he saw things from God's standpoint he was not tempted by them any more. His temptation was the thought that it hardly paid to be a follower of God. The wicked seemed to get along better than he, and evidently the devil was tempting him to think that salvation did not pay. This was no doubt Solomon's trouble in the days of his vanity. He saw the righteous perishing in his righteousness, and he saw the wicked prolonging his days in his wickedness. Then the temptation would be that there was no profit in salvation.

These same things obtain to-day; some **righteous** people are in poverty and suffering, and in it all they die; while some wicked people live in luxury and worldly prosperity, and in that they die. Looking at things from a purely worldly standpoint one might think that it does not pay to be a Christian; but from the standpoint of heaven the view is entirely changed, as David soon saw. So, Solomon, seeing the state and latter end of both the righteous and the wicked, and judging things from his standpoint of vanity, it would be perfectly natural for him to say that there is no use in putting too much stress on righteousness, for the righteous do not seem to get along any better, or even so well, as the wicked. But his godly training would not permit him to throw away all desire to be right; yet, feeling there would be no special benefit in any great quantity of righteousness, he says, in the language of the text: "Be not righteous over much; neither make thyself over wise; why shouldest thou destroy thyself?" And yet, not wanting to cast too much reflection upon the possession of righteousness, he evidently tries to even it up in the next verse by saying: "Be not over much wicked; neither be thou foolish (just the opposite condition to his former statement); why shouldest thou die before thy time?" I suppose Solomon thought, in his unregenerate state of vanity, that he was keeping "in the middle of the road." He did not think it best to get too much religion, or to be too wicked. If we mistake not, there are many of his order still living.

Do not let the reader forget that this statement was the thought of Solomon in the days of his vanity, when he did not know any better.

To take this text to prove the possibility of being too righteous certainly shows ridiculousness in the extreme. Yet it has been done; how much we do not know. In Adam Clarke's time he cites a case, and says: "It cannot be supposed, except by those who are entirely unacquainted with the nature of true religion, that a man may have *too much holiness; too much of the life of God in his soul*. And yet a learned Doctor, in three sermons on this text, has endeavored to show, out-doing Solomon's infidel, 'the sin, folly and danger of being righteous over much.' O rare darkness!"

CHAPTER XVIII.

A JUST MAN FALLETH SEVEN TIMES.

"For a just man falleth seven times, and riseth up again; but the wicked shall fall into mischief." —*Prov. 24:16.*

From the way some quote this text to justify their continual sinning, it seems that they have found comfort in it. If it means what some think it does, it certainly is very discouraging for the future of all Christians. If the work of Christ's redemption cannot do more than to let one "fall seven times a day," as it is generally quoted, and fall into sin, as is supposed, then we do not see much advantage of the follower of Christ over the unregenerate world. Is this the best Christ can do for a child of God? Is this the condition of His real followers? Then where is the blessedness of salvation? Indeed, where is salvation at all?

If this text means that the just man falls into sin seven times a day, and the words of the apostle John are true where he says, "He that committeth sin is of the devil," then seven times a day a just man is of the devil. How would one of these pleaders for sin feel if one should say to him, "I am sorry for you, my brother, for I am persuaded that seven times a day on the average, you are really of the devil." We wonder if he would believe the statement. We feel sure that he would resent it. The fact is, the text is not only misquoted, but misunderstood. It is something like the one some try to quote from Job 5:7. They say, "Man is prone to evil as the sparks fly upward." The Word neither says that, nor means that. It says: "Yet man is born unto trouble (*labor*, see margin), as the sparks fly upward." More or less trouble comes into every life, even of the holiest. Holiness is a comfort in the midst of it, but it does not exempt one from it. So, if these who pervert this text in our lesson would first read it, and then study it and the context, they would never honestly apply it in the direction they do.

It might be a matter of information to some to learn that there are two words wanting in the text which are supposed by many to be there; one written and the other inferred, viz., the word "day" and the word "sin." Neither of these words are there, either by inference or by writing. What right has any one to say *seven times a day*, when there is nothing of the kind stated? One has no more right to say seven times *a day* than seven times *a second*. There is no time stated at all. As to the sin question, it is simply carnal, human conjecture. There is not the shadow of proof that it implies sin. To say that it means sin is to fly in the face of the inspired Word of God, and discount the power and atonement of Jesus Christ. Thank God we have a better understanding of the Word, and a better appreciation of the work and willingness and power of our Christ. We wonder that these who have such an estimate of the work of Christ as to believe the best He has for us is a constantly sinning religion, do not give up in hopeless despair. Probably their belief in "the final perseverance of the saints," as some have thought the text to mean, buoys them up and on in their (sinful) way.

A little thought and study of the Word will convince one that there are more ways to fall than into sin. James says: "My brethren, count it all joy when ye fall." Now, if to fall means necessarily to fall into sin, and if one follows James' instruction to count it all joy, the one who sins the most frequently would then be in possession of the most joy. What a joyful set then the worst sinners in the world ought to be! But James shows us that we may fall into something else besides sin. "My brethren, count it all joy when ye fall into divers temptations." The reason why we should count it all joy is because, as he adds in the next verse, "Knowing this, that the trying of your faith worketh patience." Patience is something worth possessing, and when we fall into different kinds of temptations we should rejoice at the result, which is more patience, if we constantly look to Christ.

David once said, when he got into trouble: "Let

A Just Man Falleth Seven Times. 149

us fall now into the hand of the Lord; for His mercies are great; and let me not fall into the hand of man." Thus, we see from the foregoing Scriptures, that there may be a falling into temptation, a falling into the hand of God, and a falling into the hand of man. Other places show that one may "fall into mischief," "fall into a ditch," "in time of temptation fall away," "fall into the condemnation of the devil." How are we to ascertain, then, what kind of a fall it is, when the text simply mentions the fall, without stating the nature of it? We know of no better way than to take up the context.

In the text before us we read that "A just man falleth seven times," but it does not say what the fall is, or where it is. The same text mentions another fall, and says what that is: "The wicked shall fall into mischief." This is certainly a different fall from that of the righteous, because it follows the word "but," which indicates something opposite or different from the preceding statement. So, we know that the falling of the righteous here does not mean into mischief. Let us see the previous verse in the context. "Lay not wait, O wicked man, against the dwelling of the righteous; spoil not his resting place." We see then that the righteous may suffer at the hands of the wicked. The words "righteous" and "just" mean the same thing here. He may be distressed in his resting place; he may have it all broken up; the wicked may lie in wait for him, as we read so often in the Word; he may fall many times into the hands of such men. So, when the statement is made that "a just man falleth seven times," we may know of a certainty that it means a falling into affliction, or some calamity, or trouble, at the hands of the wicked. Adam Clarke says that the word here translated to fall is never applied to sin. Such falling may come to any Christian. Indeed, the apostle Paul assures us that "All that will live godly in Christ Jesus shall suffer persecution." We may expect to suffer it in the manner mentioned in the text. And, instead of it being in favor of a sinning religion, it shows the possibilities of a salvation far beyond anything of the kind. In falling into these distresses we see that he has the power to rise again. Thank God there is nothing in this world that can come between the righteous soul and Christ to overthrow him, if he looks to Christ for help. God has provided grace sufficient to keep one under all circumstances. Paul wrote to a certain people, stating that they took joyfully the spoiling of their goods. So, when the wicked lie in wait against the dwelling of the righteous to spoil his resting place, we see that in falling into this distressing condition we may even rejoice, and be assured that we can rise out of it. Though we fall thus seven times, God will give us grace and power to rise. In the following verse we read: "Rejoice not when thine enemy falleth, and let not thine heart be glad when he stumbleth." Why not rejoice when this happens? Because he has none to help him out again. O the advantage of the righteous over the wicked! Surely it pays to be a Christion.

CHAPTER XIX.

I HAVE SEEN AN END OF ALL PERFECTION.

"I have seen an end of all perfection; but Thy commandment is exceeding broad."—Psalm 119: 96.

This text seems to be thrown in without any reference to anything going before or following after. There being no reference to any particular kind of perfection in connection with this statement, it is difficult to ascertain just what the Psalmist had in his mind. It is evident that he had no reference to the failure of what we call Christian perfection, for that would be directly in contradiction to the Word of God in other places. It would also contradict his own statements concerning himself in another psalm, where he says: "I will behave myself wisely in a perfect way. O when wilt Thou come unto me? I will walk within my house with a perfect heart."— Ps. 101:2. Those who would base an argument against holiness upon this isolated text are certainly pressed for proof; and yet, with some it seems that anything that has the least shadow of a hint that way is grasped as a drowning man grasps for a straw. We are reminded of the story that is told concerning one of Robert G. Ingersoll's

I Have Seen an End of All Perfection. 153

lectures. While he was ridiculing the fact of there being a hell, one of his drunken listeners called out, saying: "Make it strong, Bob; a good many of us are depending on you."

Why should any one want any argument or statement to encourage him to remain in sin when God has provided a way to be saved to the uttermost? Why seek to find a flaw or failure in Christian perfection when God has opened up a way to give us this very grace, without which no man shall see the Lord?—Heb. 12:14.

When we read anything about perfection in the Word, before we criticise, would it not be a good idea to find out just what kind of perfection is meant? We think if our critics would adopt this plan with the text before us they would wait a long time before criticising, for probably very few who are finding fault with the doctrine on account of this text understand its meaning. We feel free to say this, for, with many scholars, this meaning is a matter of disagreement. We think a note from the writings of Daniel Steele will throw the needed light upon this misunderstood text. The following is from him:

"No text in the Old Testament is more frequently quoted against Christian perfection, usually with an air of triumph, as though that doctrine is pulverized by the crushing momentum of this verse. Let us examine it. The original for perfection in this passage is a once-used word in the

Hebrew Bible. Hence, its meaning is with scholars a matter of dispute. But many of them agree that it is the complete ending and vanishing away of anything. Thus, Martin Luther renders it, 'I have seen an end of all things, but Thy law lasts.' Hence, the word perfection, not being in their version, the Germans have no difficulty with the text. All earthly things end, but the Bible lasts. The rendering makes the text concordant with Isa. 40: 6-8, and I Pet. 1:24-25, "All flesh is as grass; the grass withereth, and the flower thereof falleth away; but the word of the Lord endureth forever." That the idea of this text in the alphabetical psalm is the evanescence of the earthly and the eternity of the spiritual, especially of divine revelation, is proven by the Septuagint version: "I have seen the end of every finishing up; but Thy commandment is very wide;" while the Vulgate reads: *"Omnis consummationis finem vidi;"* literally, "I have seen the end of every consummation." We confidently make the assertion that no candid scholar, however strong his prejudices against evangelical perfection, or loving God with all the heart, after a thorough study of this text, will ever again hurl it against the precious, Scriptural doctrine and blessed, conscious experience of myriads of His saints."—*Daniel Steele, in "Half Hours With St. Paul."*

CHAPTER XX.

SUMMARY.

As a matter of simple reference, we append the following synopsis, so that one may, in a moment, get the thought of any of these perverted texts without having to read a whole chapter:

"If we say that we have no sin, we deceive ourselves, and the truth is not in us."—I John 1:8.

This does not mean the one who has received the experience of the preceding verse, wherein "the blood of Jesus Christ His Son cleanseth us *from all sin,*" but it has reference to one who has not received the cleansing, and, while he has sin in him, declares that he has *no* sin.

"As it is written, There is none righteous, no, not one."—Rom. 3:10.

There is no one in his natural, unregenerate state that is righteous. When God puts salvation into one's heart He pronounces that one righteous, as is seen in numerous instances in the Word. Referring to the places where "it is written," one can readily see the class of people mentioned, among which "There is none righteous, no, not one."

"For there is no man that sinneth not."—1 Kings 8:46; I Chron. 6:36.

"For there is not a just man upon earth, that doeth good, and sinneth not."—Eccl. 7:20.

As is shown by the Bible exegetes, these verses in the original do not teach that all men are sinners, nor that all men sin; but using in the translation the potential mood, which is wanting in the Hebrew language, it would read, *"may not sin,"* instead of reading, *"sinneth not."* It does not teach the necessity of sinning, but rather the possibility of sinning.

"Not as though I had already attained, either were already perfect."—Phil. 3:12.

We know that Paul here did not mean that he was lacking in Christian perfection, for he mentions the fact in the fifteenth verse that he has the experience. He simply alludes to the fact that he has not that resurrection perfection (see verse 12) for which he is looking with joyful expectancy. Knowing that, "Blessed and holy is he that hath part in the first resurrection," he is desirous to be among those that shall have a resurrection out from among the dead, and so be in the first resurrection. Such will be the experience of the holy ones.

"If I say, I am perfect, it shall also prove me perverse."—Job 9:20.

Job is not discountenancing perfection either in

himself or in any one else. He is not casting any slur upon the testimony of that experience. He is not disclaiming the experience. He is simply making the statement that if he should claim perfection as a reason why he should not suffer affliction it would prove him perverse. Job's "comforters" had been telling him that he was suffering so because he was such a sinner; but he was letting them know that they were not correct, and yet he would not plead perfection as a reason for exemption from suffering. Even if Job did not think himself to be perfect, as some would assert, the Lord settled that question before, by saying in the first verse of the book that he was perfect.

"This is a faithful saying, and worthy of all acceptation, that Christ Jesus came into the world to save sinners, of whom I am chief."—I. Tim. 1:15.

If Paul meant that he was the chief of sinners at the time of this writing, it certainly contradicts his other statements concerning his Christian experience. What he declares here is, that he, being the chief of sinners, "obtained mercy" (see verse 16), thus proving the faithful saying that Christ Jesus came into the world to save sinners. He was the chief sinner saved, and not the chief sinner after he was saved.

"Who can say, I have made my heart clean, I am pure from my sin?"—Prov. 20:9.

No one can truthfully say that he has made his heart clean, or that he is pure from his sin by anything that he has done, except to come to the Lord and comply with the conditions of salvation, and let God do the work. Salvation comes from the Lord. It is not by human effort, nor by good works, nor by moral living. Salvation means life, and without the "power of an endless life" no one will ever reach heaven. When God makes one's heart clean and purifies him from sin it is well to notify others of this great fact, so that they may make application for the same blessed work of grace.

The seventh chapter of Romans is a picture of a Jew, probably Paul himself, under the law, without grace, trying to do the right, and failing therein, proving conclusively that no one is able in and of himself to save himself, or bring himself into a satisfied experience.

It was not Paul's experience at the time of that writing, because he wrote immediately afterwards the eighth chapter, which shows the blessed deliverance and victory, and both experiences could not have been his at the same time; or, in other words, at the time he wrote the epistle. It was not Paul's experience in a justified state, for that would make the Word of God contradict itself, according to the teaching of the apostle John in the first epistle, third chapter, and eighth and ninth verses. Some of the expressions, though, used by Paul in this chapter express the struggles of the justified believer prior to sanctification.

"And lest I should be exalted above measure through the abundance of the revelations, there was given to me a thorn in the flesh, a messenger of Satan to buffet me, lest I should be exalted above measure."—II Cor. 12:7.

That any one should suppose for a moment that this thorn was carnality is simply ridiculous. He received it at the time of the revelations; then he did not have it before. This settles the carnality question.

Weighing all the evidence in the case, we have no doubt that it was a mangled facial condition. At the time of his stoning at Lystra, he no doubt received injuries about the face and eyes that made it most embarrassing to him in his work, and made it necessary for him to have constant assistance in the great work devolving upon him.

The statements of Job's "comforters," mentioned in chapter ten, when properly understood, do not prove by inspiration that God puts no trust in His servants; that He charges His angels with folly; that man cannot be clean; that the heavens are not clean in His sight, and that the stars are not pure. These statements should never be quoted to prove the sinful condition of God's children. The testimony of Job, who was a perfect man, and the testimony of the Lord, was that these men did not always speak the right things. Surely, in these statements, they did not speak that which was right. Hence, their words here, instead of being the inspired words from the Lord, were evidently of their own mind, and not correct.

"And He said unto him, Why callest thou me good? There is none good but one, that is, God."—Matt. 19:17.

It does not mean that there are no good people in the world, even in grace, for that would contradict the statements where good people are mentioned. To say that there are none good in their natural state would harmonize with the teaching in other places, where we learn that "There is none righteous, no, not one," and "There is none that doeth good, no, not one." To say that no one is good, in the absolute sense, but God, would harmonize with the Word throughout. Hence, the Word teaches that there are people who are good, made so by grace; that in their unregenerate state there are none good; that none, even in the highest state of grace, are good in the absolute sense; this belongs to God only.

"Who shall change our vile body, that it may be fashioned like unto His glorious body?"—Phil. 3:21.

The Revised Version makes this text plain. Instead of saying *"vile body,"* it says *"the body of our humiliation."* We see, then, that it has no reference to a sinful or corrupt body, but simply to the body of our humble state in this world before the glorified state beyond.

"I die daily."—*I Cor.* 15:31.

This verse does not have any reference to dying more and more unto sin. It has no reference to any further dying to self or deeper crucifixions after one is sanctified, as so many quote it to mean. The apostle Paul is simply calling attention to the fact that he is in danger of losing his earthly life any day. The continued persecutions, the liability of being thrown in with wild beasts, or the danger of meeting death in some other way, was constantly staring him in the face. Hence, in view of all this, he said, "I die daily." In other words, "My life is in jeopardy daily."

"Be ye angry, and sin not."—*Eph.* 4:26.

This is no license to get mad. It is no license to have "righteous indignation," which makes one act the same as other people do when they get mad. Instead of it being a command to be angry in some proper sense, or a permission for it, it is just the opposite—it is a prohibiton. The true thought, then, is, "Be not ye angry, lest ye commit sin." Or, by emphasizing the last word *"not,"* we get the true meaning: "Be ye angry, and sin not." It must mean this, or we make the context contradict this verse. In the context a little further on we read that we must put away anger. Of course, the inspired apostle would not tell us in one verse to do something, and then right afterwards tell us to put away that same thing.

"Forgive us our sins."—Luke 11:4. *"Forgive us our debts."—Matt.* 6:12.

Whoever does wrong should confess it and pray for forgiveness. Whether it is a known sin or a sin of ignorance, application to God for pardon should be made. That it is necessary for one to sin knowingly day by day, the prayer does not teach. That everybody in any state of grace will do things ignorantly, which afterwards they may see, we all know, and as all these things will throw one into debt to God, he should pray the prayer that the Lord taught His disciples. True, the disciples were, before Pentecost, in a state where they were much more liable to sin in various ways than after Pentecost. Even the Pentecostal experience will not free one from mistakes, blunders, misjudgments, and some other human frailties.

"But I keep under my body, and bring it into subjection; lest that by any means, when I have preached to others, I myself should be a castaway."—1 *Cor.* 9:27.

Paul kept his physical being in subjection; he

was the master, and not his *body*. He had no reference to carnality, the body of sin, for he says in Rom. 6:6 that such was destroyed. He means his physical nature, together with its attributes of appetites, passions, desires, which, if kept in the place that God intended them to be, would be holy and right; but if allowed to get out of their proper sphere would be corrupt and sinful. Ecery sanctified soul should do as Paul did—keep his body under.

"Be not righteous over much; neither make thyself over wise; why shouldest thou destroy thyself?"—Eccl. 7:16.

This is not a command against Pharisaical pretentions to piety. It does not teach that it is possible to become too righteous. In the preceding verse we learn that the statement was made in the days of Solomon's vanity. The thought is that Solomon, before he knew the way of salvation, saw the state of the righteous, and also the state of the wicked; and from his carnal view he could not see wherein it paid to be very righteous; so he said, "Be not righteous over much." He did not feel free to throw aside all righteousness, but thought that it might be best to "keep in the middle of the road." This thought was in the days of his vanity, and not at the time of writing that text.

"For a just man falleth seven times, and riseth up again."—Prov. 24:16.

There is no thought of sin in the text. The word *"sin"* is not mentioned, as so many seem to think it is. Placing this alongside of the previous text we learn that the wicked may bring calamity upon the just; through the wickedness of the wicked the righteous fall into trouble and calamity seven times; but out of it all they rise again.

"I have seen an end of all perfection; but Thy commandment is exceeding broad."—Psalm 119: 96.

It does not mean that he has seen an end of Christian perfection, nor the failure of it in any way, for the Word of God does not thus contradict itself; and the psalmist himself believed differently in his own experience. Evidently the thought is, that there is an end of all earthly things, but the spiritual, the things of God, are eternal, ever abiding.

CHAPTER XXI.

CONCLUSION.

To say that there are no apparent contradictions in the Word regarding the life of holiness would be false. To say there are *real* discrepancies would likewise be false. God's word does not contradict itself. Even if some apparently opposite statements are found we should exercise as much wisdom as faithful jurors in a court. They weigh the evidence of both sides, and decide in favor of the preponderance. Would it not be wise on our part to do the same? While there are some places in the Scriptures which seem, without investigation, to indicate the impossibility of living a holy life here, yet there are multiplied times as many which make positively clear the very opposite. Shall we not decide according to the preponderance of evidence?

God commands us to be holy; to be perfect in our sphere as Christians, as He is perfect in His sphere as God. We are to fill our sphere as Christians as God fills His sphere as God. We cannot be perfect gods, but we can be perfect Christians. To demand any more than this, such as absolute perfection, would make His commands transcend our ability to perform; to demand any less, would be inconsistent with His moral government. The standard of salvation, then, could not be different without interfering with the essential attributes of God, viz., mercy on the one hand, and justice on the other.

We have been astonished at intelligent men—yea, ministers of the Gospel—astonished at the way they handle the Word of God in regard to this sin question. Only to-day we ran across a book of Bible Readings, written by a minister of the Gospel, and under the chapter entitled "Why Does the Christian Sin?" we copy the following, word for word:

"We wish to do the right, but we do the evil. The old man is alive still, and he finds a rival. There is war (Rom. 7:23). Here are two natures existing side by side in the Christian: the evil inciting to evil, the good urging to good.

"First John 3:9 is true as it stands; it is the idea in the original. We must not attempt to explain it away, for it is, evidently, spoken not of the old man, but of the new, that which is born of God. It is, therefore, like God, and cannot sin. Sin is of the devil; the old nature is as he is, loving sin.

"This might be illustrated to a slight extent by the process of grafting. Take a wild peach tree, put in a graft from the Crawford variety, and the graft will bear Crawford peaches. The graft is the insertion of a new nature; it is not intended as an improvement of the wild peach, but to produce a widely different result. The old stock will send out shoots; these, if allowed to grow, will bear bitter peaches, so that at the same time you would have bitter and sweet fruit on the same tree. The Crawford branch cannot bear bitter fruit, neither can the old stock bear the luscious Crawford. So in man's new nature, he cannot, he does not, sin; but in his old he does. Forgiveness of sins does not affect the nature that produces the sin; it will continue to incite to evil until a separation is made in death between the spiritual and carnal.

"What advantage, then, hath the Christian? He cries out, Who shall deliver from this dead body? (Rom. 7:24.) Christ delivers. (Rom. 6:6-8.) 'Our old man is crucified with Him.' 'If we be dead with Christ, we believe that we shall also live with Him.' Col. 3:3 makes it more forcible; "Ye are dead.' As far as God's law is concerned, we are dead. What is true of our Vicar, is true of us. He died, so there is, therefore, no condemnation, because we are, in Him, united by adoring faith. God does not look to the believer for a satisfaction to violated law; that He seeks from our Substitute, our Daysman, our Shield, our Righteousness. We are accepted in the Beloved; we are imperfect in ourselves, but in Him complete.

"What are we to do when we sin? Go to the Father. He is faithful, just; He forgives and cleanses. He is glad to do it. (Luke 15.) Then 'reckon ye yourselves to be dead unto sin, but alive unto God through Jesus Christ our Lord.' 'Let

not sin, therefore, reign in your mortal body.'
'Grow in grace'."

Here we have the anti-holiness doctrine in a nut shell. It is a real epitome of the error which we have to meet from day to day. If it had been written on purpose to show how much beautiful error could be condensed into a given space, we do not see how it could be improved. It is a typical rendering of the monstrous heresies of the last days. We do not want to pass it by without pointing out some of its errors. By so doing we show forth some leading delusions of holiness skeptics.

1. *It teaches sanctification at death.* It simply assumes the thought and gives no "thus saith the Lord" at all. The whole thing of death sanctification is mere assumption and presumption. Why should one build up a system of belief without a word of Scripture to back it up?

2. *It teaches that carnality is in the physical instead of the spiritual being.* The great deliverance is to come, according to the statement made, when the spiritual is separated from the carnal at death. Now, the only separation that takes place at death is between the body and the spirit. If, then, we are to be delivered from carnality only at death, we are shut up to the delusion that carnality is located in the physical, and not the spiritual being. This doctrine was certainly obtained somewhere outside the Word of God, for there is no teaching in the Bible to substantiate such a notion.

3. *It teaches an imputed holiness only; Christ's robe of righteousness covering up our sins, and God accepting His perfection and paying no attention to our imperfections.* We think the devil would not want anything better than to make one feel that he has a standing in Christ, and could now sin, and God would take no notice of it.

4. *It teaches that our new nature, that which is born of God, does not sin, but that our old nature does sin.* The Crawford graft will produce luscious Crawford peaches, but the old, wild stalk will keep bearing the bitter peaches. If the new nature *did* sin, we wonder what kind of sin it would be. We wonder if it would resemble the old kind. "But," say they, "the new man cannot sin." Then some part of us after regeneration is certainly relieved of free moral agency. It has no power to do wrong. It is simply a spiritual machine, relieved of all power of choice. Volition, then, does not exist. Such imbecility of thought is disgusting!

The old stalk will keep on sinning, and the new graft will be all right. So, if one has the new graft, no matter if the old stalk does keep throwing up the old kind of shoots, he is a Christian just the same! Let us see if this will hold good. Suppose that old, wild peach tree had been in the habit of bearing such fruit as theft, lying, adultery, etc., and now, after receiving the new graft, and becoming a Christian, that same **fruit of** stealing, lying and committing adultery should be seen on its branches, what would the believers of such a doctrine think? Would they say, "O, he is a Christian all right; that is simply the old man; the new man would not, could not, do such thiugs." But I think I hear some of them say, "No, if he was seen doing such things we would know that he had never had the new man." Then where are we to draw the line? Sin is sin, and while these just mentioned would indicate that the new man was wanting, would not other sins indicate the same? We would think the old, wild peach tree, if it bore fruit at all, would be likely to bear the same kind it did before. The fact is, the thing will not hold together. The law does not, if it has been transgressed, punish the old nature and let the new nature go; it punishes the man. Salvation changes the man, and he that was a sinner before is a changed man now, and saved from his old life of sin. It is true he has, till sanctified, the old man, but that does not have sway; it is controlled, and does not bear sinful fruit. God proposes to rid us of this element, and fill us with His Holy Spirit, and renovate us through and through.

5. *It teaches us to reckon ourselves to be dead indeed unto sin when we are not dead indeed.* It teaches us to reckon what is not true. It simply means for us to reckon a lie. This erroneous doctrine is everywhere in Christendom. The idea of reckoning a lie! Does not the Word warn us

against the danger of believing a lie? They say, "The old man is not dead, but we are to reckon him as dead." The thing we want, though, is his death. Simply reckoning a thing dead does not kill it. But if we fulfill the conditions of full salvation as laid down in the Word, so that God can come in and perform the execution of the old man, and then in faith reckon ourselves to be "dead indeed unto sin," we shall find that our dead reckoning will prove correct; otherwise it will prove a delusion.

6. *It teaches that sin will keep coming up, but as fast as it comes the blood will cleanse.* That is, sin is like an old sore which cannot be eliminated, but the best that can be done is, when it pours out its impurity, let it be washed off. The blood cleanses from all sin, but only as fast as it makes its appearance. Such a doctrine! This is really what some believe. We feel like writing in connection with such nonsense, *Ultima Thule,* for certainly it seems to be the jumping-off place.

7. *It brings up the seventh chapter of Romans to prove the impossibility of sin eradication now.* We wonder what Paul would think, if he were living, if he should hear all those who pervert his plain teaching, and say at the same time, "My experience is like the apostle Paul's." There lies before me just now a paper in which is written an article describing a great holiness revival meeting. The pastor of one of the leading churches of the

great city in which the revival was being held, arose and made some kind remarks concerning the wonderful meetings, stating that God was with the people, and finally added: "I have not the experience that many of you claim; I am like Paul; 'I have not apprehended;' but I bid you God-speed from my heart." The thought is, he was not sanctified as some of them claimed to be; he was like Paul. That is, Paul was not sanctified, consequently was not so far in the Christian life as they claimed to be. "Wrested Scriptures!" How they are twisted and wrung from their intended meaning!

8. *It teaches verily, that the atonement of Christ is a partial failure.* If sin has got so hidden away in the recesses of our nature that it cannot be eradicated till death, and if it is true that only as it is left in this mortal body, when the spirit goes to God, can we be free from it, then certainly the atonement cannot reach it, and so must be at least a partial failure. What an insult to Christ! Thank God we have learned the better way.

The whole thing is a bundle of contradictions and perverted Scriptures. It lays itself liable to the criticism that the Christian has no advantages over the sinner, and then tries to prove that he has, but fails to make it clear, simply putting it on a false hope of dead reckoning, which is very dead indeed.

Peter tells us there are some Scriptures which

people wrest unto "their own destruction." There seems to be no place where this is more apparent than in connection with the subject of full salvation. As salvation is the most important thing in the world, and holiness is the fulness of this most important thing, we see then how clearly one may wrest these blessed Scriptures bearing upon this great salvation, with tremendous havoc to the soul. Are there not wrecks everywhere, that once were clearly saved? All because they rejected the light of holiness. When the children of Israel failed to pass on from Kadesh-Barnea into the Promised Land, instead of remaining at that sacred spot (Kadesh means holiness), they turned their backs upon Canaan and went into the "howling wilderness," and their bleached bones lined the trail of their wanderings till the whole army, above twenty years of age, save Caleb and Joshua, had perished by the way. So it is to-day. When God calls the convert from the border land of the Canaan of perfect love, and he refuses to respond to the call, he will surely, and soon, forfeit his justification, and his spiritual bones will bleach by the wayside. O the spiritually dead carcasses that are seen all over this fair land of ours, simply because they failed to go in and "possess the land?" And why did they not go in? One great reason is, because they were not careful with the Word of God, but rather wrested it from its true meaning, and then **hid under the refuge of lies thus formed,** securing for themselves "their own destruction."

Some of the very texts thus wrested and made to bring such a curse to their souls, when properly understood, are the very ones calculated to assist in leading one on into the light of holiness. How sad to think that what God intended for light should be used for darkness; that what He intended for a help should be turned into a hindrance; that what He meant to bless should be made a curse; that what He meant for a life of holiness should be construed to mean a life of sin! O the disappointment some must be to Christ! What a disappointment some will be to their own souls! What an awful wail will come up at the last great day! "Herein is our *love made perfect* (experience of holiness), that we may have boldness at the day of judgment." (I John 4:17). If we fail in receiving this love, or if we forfeit the same, then may we expect to lack the judgment day preparation. God bless the holiness movement. God bless the faithful witnesses of holiness. God help the Christians seeking for the light. God pity those who are turning their light into darkness, and wresting His truth unto their souls' destruction. Let us be true to God, true to His Word, true to each other, and true to ourselves. We shall soon be through with this world; let us have the experience, and live the life we shall wish we had, when we face the stern realities of the other world. Amen.

www.ingramcontent.com/pod-product-compliance
Lightning Source LLC
Chambersburg PA
CBHW031353040426
42444CB00005B/269